Inside Hawai`i Prison Walls

Psychological, Moral Reasoning, and Relational Attachment.

Books by Dr. Shirley J. Davenport

Moving Beyond Denial Into Recovery:
An Educational Life Changing Workbook

Inside Hawai`i Prison Walls

Psychological, Moral Reasoning, and Relational Attachment.

Dr. Shirley Davenport, Psychologist

DELANE PUBLISHING

ISBN 13
978-0-9977593-0-3
1. Psychology 2. Spirituality 3. Self Help

First Edition: May 15, 2017

Cover Design by Stacy Comer
Typesetting by Saforabu Graphix
Front cover photo: © Ericbvd | Depositphotos.com

Published by Delane Publishing
P.O. Box 195, Wailuku, Maui, HI 96793 USA

Published in the United States of America

Printed in USA

Acknowledgements

I acknowledge with my gratitude my wonderful husband and his support for the encouragement during this learning process beginning in 1983. Calvin, thank you for your unconditional love. So not to be remiss, my gratefulness is extended to members of my support group, for their understanding while I devoted time in pursuing my dream.

To my mother, Josephine W. Brown, whose only dream was to have one of her ten children earn a college degree. Mom, with the help of God, your dream has become a reality. To the rest of my family, I thank you for your encouragement and love. I owe special thanks to my friends for encouraging me to return to school. Thank you for believing in me. Thank you, Shela Cox, for helping with editing and countless hours of proofreading.

I also thank Mark Patterson, Warden of the Women's Community Correctional Center, whose approval made it possible to work within the facility. Thank you, Chaplain Tammy and inmates, for all your help. Thank you, to each of the women for your excitement and willingness to openly share your experiences with me.

Finally, special thanks to Dr. David Rentler, Psy.D., and Dr. Deborah Simmons, Ph.D. for being a part of my team. To my committee chair and mentor, Dr. Kathryn Kelly, Ph.D., thank you for your willingness to mentor me, keep me on track, and for being my anti-anxiety cure. I could never thank you enough for your feedback and guidance. With a special extended gratitude to my publisher Dr. Ayin Adams.

Contents

Preface

The direct cost to taxpayers in the United States annually from 2011 is approximate $75 billion with continuing increases. The estimated cost to the state of Hawai'i annually just to house criminals in federal, state, and private correctional facilities are approximate $65 million during the same time frame.

Since 2010, I have had the privilege of serving professionally in the arena of public safety, corrections, and with the homeless populations. It has indeed been an honor to serve parolees in a residential relapse prevention program, as well as going to the prison to teach classes in drama and smart recovery. It has truly been an awesome experience to witness many positive outcomes among the women offenders with who I have seen faith-based spiritual encounters. The phenomena of spirituality have proven the most complete, holistic, and inclusive design for living for this protected population. Therefore, my main goal of writing this book is to educate and inform policymakers to give hope to the women who are behind prison walls. I have seen, and I do believe that changing the hearts and cognitive schemas of people are essential to changing their behaviors.

Inside Hawai'i Prison Walls: Beyond Rehabilitation Psychological, Moral Reasoning, Emotional Relational Attachment is the phenomena of spiritual bankrupt, unresolved psychological, social and health issues among Incarcerated Women in Hawai`i. Like all humans, Women go through stages. Women grow up in the social environment which they inherit from society. Many women are caught up in situations and lifestyles during their life cycle in which they often wonder how did I get here, when did I go wrong, and what happened to me? Girls, women, and people in general often experience many forms or ways of experiencing incarceration. Women who feel spiritually rejected, neglected and abused as children battle with an orphan spirit, abandonment, and rejection. These are women who stay in dysfunctional relationships, who are caught up in addiction, and who arrive in incarceration.

Introduction

My reasons for writing this book links on my belief that spirituality is a relationship with a power greater than ourselves that strategy is the most efficient strategy for assisting women offenders. As well as other individuals in breaking through psychological, social, spiritual and physical issues in their lives today. The burdens of our society with the cost of social control systems such as welfare, prisons, and the war on drugs hurt everyone. I believe that the search should be real in finding restorative, rehabilitative, and transformational systems to help disenfranchised populations like the homeless, incarcerated, and addictive populations. The currents systems and approaches are inadequate for those who are living with economic, emotional, social, spiritual, moral, and ethical transgression problems.

Many individuals and communities practice some form of religion or spirituality to give meaning, purpose, and value to their lives. It is no secret that women are at a disadvantage when compared to men in our society. I am writing this book to share my findings, to bring understanding to the essence of spirituality, and the role spirituality plays in the lives of incarcerated women and their restoration or rehabilitation.

Serval incarcerated wahines in Hawai'i shared their belief of spirituality and its role in their lives are relational driven. Their spirituality or the lack of spirituality is due to their traditional and cultural beliefs. They need spiritual growth to achieve restoration in the form of rehabilitation and transformation. The perspectives involving spirituality includes having a relationship with divine beings or forces, such as a relationship with the "Aina" (land), as well as learning universal laws of serving others, and being committed and consistent in inward and outward intentional growth. As you read, you will become familiar with four common themes: the perception of spirituality as a relationship, the lack of a relationship with God, the desire to change attitudes and behaviors, and a transformation of the heart, soul, and mind.

The life experiences of female offenders differ significantly from that of male delinquents. The pattern of offending and the methods for rehabilitating women criminals also vary. Nedderman, Underwood, and Hardy (2010) suggest that traditional programming such as confrontational therapeutic groups oriented toward the rehabilitation of male offenders is insufficient for the rehabilitation of women offenders.

Correctional Institutions define rehabilitation as inmates' successful completion of programs that allow criminals to address risk factors that lead to both incarceration and recidivism. These programs focus on various issues such as self-efficacy, self-confidence, education, vocation, addiction, mental illness, relationships and parenting skills. Siberman (2007) reports that incarcerated women are expected and required to complete various therapeutic programs that address criminal behavior, social, environmental, and psychological issues.

The processes and the deliveries of services' outcomes among offenders have focused primarily on male offenders while neglecting the rehabilitative services appropriate for women offenders. Historically, research in criminology and sociology has overlooked the complicated and intricate lives of incarcerated women. Consideration must be made for gender differences when lawmakers, public safety administration, and human services organizations are developing rehabilitation programs for female criminals. Women inmates and other women who find themselves in any form of incarceration have some challenges namely: psychological scars; education, economic, and social needs; mental illnesses and substance addictions (Anumba, Dematteo, and Heilburn, 2012).

Research by Covington and Bloom (2006) indicate that many of these issues are thought to have evolved from adverse incidents of early childhood. For example, abuse and neglect emotional, physical and sexual, along with other traumatic experiences. Nature and nurture, as well as individual risk factors (i.e., unhealthy relationships, abuse, and the lack of self-efficacy), are associated with an increased risk of incarceration and recidivism among women offenders (Anumba et al., 2012). Extensive evidence by McDaniels-Wilson and Judson (2011) suggests that abusive relationships, poverty, secondary education and vocation experiences, substance abuse, and mental illness are prevalent among women before incarcerations. Such issues are associated with the implication and impact the rate of recidivism. Recidivism has become an increasing problem for the criminal justice system and society.

The complexity of women's needs, rehabilitation, and recidivism of incarcerated women has drawn attention to the need to develop strategies for understanding and changing the nature of these offenders' behaviors and attitudes. Slattery and Park (2011) suggest that understanding human beings requires knowing their belief and value systems, as well as how individuals process and operate in the world from their cognitive and existential perspectives. The meaning systems for many people determine their beliefs, goals, and values which formed through spirituality or religion (Slattery & Parker, 2011).

Fowler, Faulkner, Learman, and Runnels (2011) defined spirituality as "a way of being, an awareness of the transcendent, beliefs," interaction with God. Practices that allow individuals to develop meanings and purposes for their lives. Work by Walton (2007) also implied that spirituality could be necessary for successfully addressing maladaptive behaviors, reducing recidivism, substance abuse in adults. As well as, an alternative education for youth. Swanson (2009) claims that an improved understanding of the essence of spirituality may be helpful in developing programs that create positive change in the behavior of incarcerated women, and may also point to factors that could foster a deeper understanding of religious differences between male and women offenders in developing rehabilitative gender-responsive programs. O'Connor and Duncan (2011) study explored the link between a humanist, spiritual, and religion pathway to life meaning, human culture, and recidivism. They conclude that "HSR pathways to meaning may be an important part of the evidence-based principle of responsiveness and resistance process" as part of lowering rates of recidivism. In a study that consisted of 3,009 first year incarcerated men, and 349 women reveal that widespread human, social and spiritual capital are naturally supportive of processes of humanist, religious, and religion responsive as well as the distancing process for thousands of men and women in returning to prison. In the sense of numbers, they found that 70% of women, 68% men and 48% of teenagers attended spiritual and religious institutions. Both women and men were equally likely to attend spiritual or religious groups as children. Men were more likely to visit before their arrest (30% compared to women at 23%). Women were more likely than men to attend in the year after their arrest (66% versus 54%). Findings like these suggest that it is important to consider gender differences and the behavior of women as separate pathways from those of men when planning correctional rehabilitation and reducing recidivism.

Sharma, Charak, and Sharma in their report also argue that transformation of negative personality characteristics is needed to move this vulnerable population toward the emergent of self-awareness, personal values, and socially acceptable behaviors. This investigation consists of focus group sessions, individual interviews with women offenders in a Prison in Hawai'i. I explored both the personality characteristics and spirituality among women offenders.

And the role of spirituality and mystical quest in bringing about a lifestyle change in the psyche, social ability, and life meaning among women inmates in Hawai'i.

Inside Hawai`i Prison Walls

Psychological, Moral Reasoning, and Relational Attachment.

SECTION ONE

Background

Compared to male offenders' women criminals are at a disadvantage in regards to rates of incarceration and recidivism. My questions are how do we help incarcerated women in changing their lives and to remaining outside of prison walls. How are we to understand and change the nature of these offenders' behaviors and attitudes? The foundation of my book comes from a qualitative phenomenological study that I completed during my doctoral studies.

My intent is to explore the essence of faith-based spirituality and the role spirituality plays in the life and rehabilitation of incarcerated women in Hawai`i by examining their spiritual beliefs. As much as we know about human beings, are we aware of their moral belief and value systems? How do they individually process and operate in the world from their own cognitive and existential perspectives?

The recruits for the exploration came from a purposeful sample of 15 inmates from the Women's Community Correctional Center in Hawai`i. Each of the women's audiotaped interview was transcribed verbatim. Moustakas (1994) phenomenological data analysis method was used to analyze the data. The results of the data analysis provided four common themes:

1. the perception of spirituality as a relationship;
2. the lack of a relationship with God;
3. the desire to change attitudes and behaviors; and
4. a transformation of the heart (soul) and mind.

The results suggest that the 15 inmates believe that spirituality and the role of spirituality in their rehabilitation are relationship-driven. The detainees' perceptions varied involving having a relationship with divine individuals or invisible forces that support learning theory and social development in how to live with universal laws (i.e., service to others, compassionate, commitment, and consistency) in an outward positive direction of living. Life meaning for some individuals and many others follow a path of spirituality or religion. Implications here are very revealing there is the need for further research using longitudinal studies.

Although any one risk factor might not be associated with the increased risk of behavioral decompensation, relapse, or returning to prison. When coupled with other risk factors (i.e., unhealthy relationships, abuse, spiritual bankruptcy, and self-efficacy), rates of decompensation, relapse, and re-offending will inevitably increase. Some important implications emerged for the development of gender-responsive in-prison curriculums that are effective in rehabilitating and reducing recidivism among women inmates.

The extensive evidence of abusive relationships, poverty, poor education and vocation experiences, substance abuse, and mental illness are present among women before imprisonment. These issues are also closely associated with the rate of recidivism. Recidivism has become an increasing problem for the criminal justice system and society.

Research has established that spirituality may be a major indicator for successfully addressing maladaptive human behavior, reducing recidivism, and substance abuse in adults. Some evidence also suggests that spirituality may be an alternative education for youth. Other individuals have defined spirituality as *mindfulness, just being, an awareness of the transcendent, beliefs,* or interaction with God. As well as, practices that allow individuals to develop meaning and purpose for their lives. The humanist, spiritual, and religion pathway to life meaning, along with other ethnographic and recidivism studies suggest that a spiritual path to life meaning may be an important part of the evidence-based principle for responsiveness to changing maladapted thinking and behavior. As well as a way of addressing lower rates of repeat offending, relapse, and decompensation.

My hope and reason for work in this book are to bring some degree of awareness and understanding to professionals, policymakers, public safety, educators, and institutions. I feel that it is imperative that we understand the essence of spirituality, its role in assigning meaning and purpose to the life of individuals and families. And in the restoration and rehabilitation of lives ripped apart due to maladapted behavior, criminal thinking and lives behind prison's walls.

Social Concerns

Building larger and overcrowded prison facilities continue to be a challenge for policymakers. The criminal justice system has reached a halt in its ability to decrease criminal recidivism within the social confines of society. Lacking the housing and rehabilitation programs for incarcerated adolescent girls and women offenders. Statistics by the Bureau of Justice (BJF) (2011) showed that criminal behavior has significant financial costs. A society burdened by the cost of incarcerating and rehabilitating criminals. Noting that these individuals are living with economic, emotional, social, spiritual, moral and ethical transgression problems, maladjusted and entangled with substance abuse (Sharma et al., 2009). Per Schmitt, Warner, and Gupta (2010), the cost to taxpayers in the United States annually is approximately 75 billion dollars. Yamane (2011), estimated that the full cost to the state of Hawai`i for housing criminals in federal, state, and private correctional facilities to be approximate $65 million annually for taxpayers. Increasingly the cost to society continues to rise as female juvenile arrest statistics in Hawai`i reveal the national arrest rate for young women was 29%. While arrest rates may be considered predictive, future rates of incarceration of women in Hawai`i (Pasko, Chesney-Lind, 2007). 40% of all juveniles arrested were female and accounted for 39% of which were offenses of drug possession. However, other crimes included assaults against family members, 40% of referred cases to family court with an additional 40% being probation cases.

Fifty percent of juvenile's offenders placed under protective supervision by the courts represent 15-20% of the juveniles' population at Hawai`i's Youth Correctional Facility (Pasko & Chesney-Lind, 2007). Researchers who focus on youth risk factors found a connection to poor developmental outcomes in adulthood. Studies by Baier, Wright (2001), found a negative association between religion and spirituality correlated to crime, delinquency, and youth antisocial behaviors. The study included 60 juveniles who demonstrated by adherence to a religion or spirituality there is an association to lower recidivism rates in crime and delinquency. Furthermore, more evident in victimless crimes such as addictions (McCullough & Willoughby, 2009). Statistics released by the Bureau of Justice Statistics (BJS) in 2013 showed a marginal decline in incarcerated populations between 2011 and 2013. A marginal decline attributed to the reduction of 28,000 offenders in California driven by the state's Realignment Act of 2011. Additional information indicates the state of Hawai`i; female incarceration rate declined from 733 inmates in 2011 to 688 inmates in 2012 - a decrease of 6.1 percent. Per the BJS (2011), Hawai`i reported an increase of 3.9% - 728 women offenders in 2010 compared to 701 women offenders in 2009.

In 2011 McDaniels-Wilson and Judson noted the criminal justice administration was often perplexed by the complex needs of female prisoners. Researchers, also indicate significant risk factors of women inmates which are ignored with repetitive and or outdated procedures, rules, practices. While rehabilitation modalities in the correctional system designed for male offenders were also used to address the needs of female offenders (Kellette & Willging, 2011). McPhail, Falvo, and Burker (2012) report previous research studies specifically focused on correctional rehabilitation programs only focused on male inmates. Based on incarceration rates - criminal behavior appears to have increased in both adolescent (juvenile) girls and adult women offenders. Scholars soon realized gender specific presented a significant new area for investigation (Matheson, 2012).

Spirituality Concerns

While most of the women that come into the prison system show up with feelings of being spiritually broken, traumatized, and betrayed by men, they do not know how to reassemble themselves nor their lives. Some incarcerated women know little or nothing about God and cannot visualize how a journey to God can help on the journey to wholeness and a life with a purpose and a life without crime.

The criminal justice administration must provide appropriate and gender-responsive programs for rehabilitating incarcerated women to aid these women with successful re-entry into the community. Restorative, rehabilitative programs and strategies must focus on decreasing the rates of recidivism, the risk factors of incarcerated women, and the financial and societal burdens experienced by taxpayers and the criminal justice system.

Is it hard to believe that human beings have a spiritual dimension, a quality that goes beyond religious affiliation that strives for inspiration, reverence, awe, meaning, and purpose? Spirituality and religion help define life's meaning and function as a primary lens through which many people identify and understand their world. The essential perspective of a spiritual confrontation with the individual self-dysfunctional characteristics could transform from negative to positive behavior that can be measurable outcomes. Gender-responsive programs that give religious and spiritual meanings to people could incorporate into many secular strategies. Faith-based focused strategies also have the potential to transform lives while addressing the cognitive, behavioral, and spiritual dimensions. Religion/spirituality has shown to have value in prison, and faith-based interventions can contribute to rehabilitation when coupled with substance abuse treatment, educational, and employment services, and opportunities for inmates leaving the criminal justice system.

A holistic approach that includes religious or spiritual meanings or both may not be appropriate for all programming or every criminal prisoner. However, a comprehensive approach may make available necessary and efficient means of helping incarcerated women to live healthier, fuller, and spiritually consistent lives without continuing to offend. Women inmates can begin to address one's emotional, psychological, educational, vocational, self-efficacy, self-esteem, and relationship issues and begin to search for life meaning without repeated criminal thinking and criminal behavior.

It is safe to say that faith challenges an individual's experience to make decisions from the internal moral fibers to influence their outward conduct. Faith and spirituality development include decisions people make daily which are consistent with behavior, peace, freedom, resistance to the old lifestyles, and to maintain connectedness with new faith and moral communities. Prayer is also a measurable construct of spirituality often used within the recovery community and prison ministries as one vital resource for helping women cope, find internal strength, and hope.

Faith-based spiritual variables such as faith, prayer, fellowship, and hope may provide alternatives to embracing an abnormal belief system associated with dysfunctional behaviors. Trust significantly associate across many measures as a factor in criminal rehabilitation. Despite the marginal significance of the relationship between having faith and committing criminal conduct, "a stable belief system can help insulate individuals against doubt and inconsistency associated with exposure to these norms and keep them more focused on maintenance of prosocial attitudes and behaviors" (Nedderman, 2010).

Increasing the capacity of spirituality and contributing to the spiritual maturity of incarcerated women may be achieved by incorporating prayer, faith, and hope at little or no cost to taxpayers, the criminal justice system, or society. One strategy that may easily integrate within rehabilitation programs is prayer. Prayer or meditation is an engaging intimacy interaction with a divine source or other in the quest for guidance and solace. In most traditional recovery and restoration programs inmates are required to participate in prayer and meditation frequently. Faith is a prerequisite for hopefulness in an individual. Hope may come from multiple sources such as friends, technology, nature, diversity, equality, other institutions, family, God, or higher power.

An individual can develop faith through interplay with three hope motives such as attachment, mastery, and survival. From a spiritual perspective, hope is necessary for an orientated belief system. Hope is not only sustained by Christians but also by Buddhists, Jews, followers of Mohammed, Hindus, and African Ifa, Australian Aborigines, Native Americans, and Hawaiians. Hope carries an associated behavior of commitment to act, characteristic of cognition (thinking) and empowerment. One could make a good case for the theory that faith and moral communities provide opportunities for practicing honest living through positive role models who supply examples of how individuals may build a relationship with God and others.

Faith-based spiritual strategies target antisocial values while focusing on accountability, responsibility, and respectability. Spirituality changes how people deal with conflict. It also provides support for developing prosocial skills of those who interact with religious or spiritual individuals or communities. Ministries such as InnerChange Freedom Initiative, the Horizon Program, and the Life Learning Program have progressively entered correctional facilities to address the challenges of restorative, rehabilitation, and recidivism issues among offenders.

Separation of Systems

Historically, the philosophy adopted by many societies was that those individuals who committed unlawful acts should receive a punishment. The use of punishment is justified in the Western judicial system. Sentence stands on the grounds of the four basic cardinal rules of retribution, deterrence, incapacitation, and rehabilitation.

1. The meaning of retribution has Biblical roots referring to "an eye for an eye. Forgiveness also has Biblical roots but is subordinate to punishment.
2. Deterrence operates from the core belief that those who see individuals punished are less likely to follow the example of the offenders.
3. The primary goal of incapacitation is to protect society by rendering offenders powerless to repeat the offenses.
4. The conceptualization of rehabilitation as the process of which successful completion of treatment or correction of criminals' maladapted behavior have equipped them to live in society and not re-offend.

While overall crime rates in the United States have decreased for the last three consecutive years (2013, 2014, and 2015), there continues to be an increase in crimes being committed by girls and women. Psychological, social, spiritual, behavioral, and other risk factors for female criminals cannot be treated in parts. Instead, it is critical to take a holistic approachn. Sixty-four percent of the inmates reported having a psychiatric disorder while 50% of the female prisoners reported having co-occurring addiction and mental illness. Therefore, the cookie-cutter approach is ineffective. In-prison programs need to be gender-responsive and holistic to address the cognitive, behavioral, emotional, spiritual, relational, and family problems of these women.

Spirituality demonstrated by a belief in God is one such program that may be able to help female inmates on several dimensions such as their psychological, moral reasoning, emotionality, and style of relational attachment. Spirituality may define life meaning, promote character change, and be beneficial for restorative, recovery-orientated thoughts and behaviors. Individuals may derive meaning from their experiences which could help bring about positive change and fulfillment in the person's life by understanding and validating faith-based spirituality values and beliefs.

Spirituality is not tangible. Spirituality is not concrete, or easily definable. Some define Spirituality as an individual search for sacred meaning. We have yet to demonstrate a direct association between spirituality and mental health counseling. However, there is a negative correlation between little or no spirituality and criminal behavior. Spirituality has been shown to be a gender-sensitive approach for reframing perception and contributing to appropriate conduct. "For I know the plans I have for you. The plans are for good and not for disaster, to give you a future and hope. So, when you pray, I will listen. If you look for me wholeheartedly, you will find me. I will end your captivity and restore your fortunes. I will gather you out of the situation and bring you home again to your land" (Jeremiah 29:11-13 NIV).

We are made of 3-Parts

Genesis Chapters 1 and 2 Creation only makes sense in light of the exodus and understood from a fundamental Developmental Psychological perspective of Biopsychosocial (Biology, Psychology, and Social Environment).

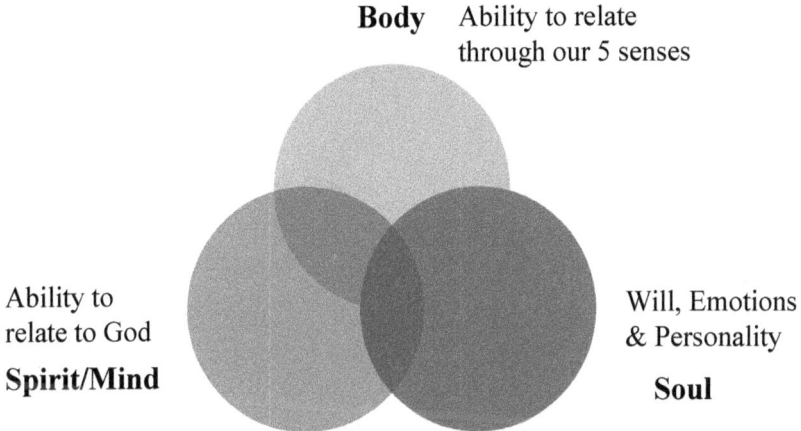

Body Ability to relate through our 5 senses

Ability to relate to God
Spirit/Mind

Will, Emotions & Personality
Soul

1. We receive information through our five senses. The physical body was created to interact with the environment in which we live. This interaction takes on acquired characteristics based on our thoughts of the situation (psychological schemas).

2. Based on the strength of one's will, emotion, and personality, the information process and passes on; our soul lives or dies (spiritual death) as a result, which may also appear in our perceptions of failure or success. We were created to be knowledgeable, rational, with the ability to communicate with God and to choose. However, we are also influenced by nurture and nature.

3. We filter the information through our souls, as well as, biological, cognitive abilities, and our environment. We have been set up to be perfect in character- capacity to think correctly and perfect in conduct to act appropriately in the spiritual realm.

SECTION TWO

Essence of Spirituality

While research shows that there is a connection between criminal behavior and spirituality, there is a limited amount of information on the subject regarding women offenders and the role of spirituality in rehabilitation, restoration, and recidivism. During a meeting with some of the women at our local women's correctional facility, two distinct questions were the focused. The aim was to understand the potential ways in which intra-psyche, self-reconciliation, and rehabilitation may be pursued by incarcerated women within a contextual essence of their lived experiences of criminality, lack of social responsibility, and spirituality.

The two questions that came to mind gave some hope to identifying the core essence of the impact of spiritual values among incarcerated women in Hawai`i. The questions may also help in discovering central patterns of processing, beliefs, values, and strategies for pursuing life meaning and purpose. So the discussion started with and was guided by (a) What are the lived experiences of incarcerated women in Hawai`i regarding spirituality? And (b) What are the lived experiences of incarcerated women in Hawai`i relating to the role of spirituality in their restoration, rehabilitation, and transformation? A limited number of books is available regarding religious/spirituality as a coping mechanism or on the effectiveness of faith-based spirituality programs among incarcerated women.

Faith-Based and Rehabilitation

Since the establishment of penitentiaries in Europe and the United States during the 1700s, public safety has always been the vital concern of the criminal justice systems in state and federal correctional facilities. The common mission of the criminal justice system has been to incapacitate criminals instead of rehabilitation. In this historical context, the philosophy was to remove criminals from society by locking them away and preventing them from committing additional crimes. The current view of the criminal justice system administrators is to protect the public and prepare criminals to be released back to the community as productive and law abiding citizens. This philosophy includes strategies for rehabilitative efforts and self-betterment efforts of individual inmates.

There is much documentation that individuals associated with religious organizations and community ministries have been providing care and support for incarcerated and paroled individuals as well as other ex-offenders. Correctional facilities are beginning to rely on faith-based and spiritual character-building as part of the inmates' rehabilitation. While there is the notion of separation of church and government, a national recognition for religious programs to address an array of social problems is on the incline.

In 2003, Lawtey Correctional Facility, one of Florida's public correctional facilities for men was the first to be converted to a faith-based program. The second facility was established in Florida one year later as the Faith- and Character-Based Institution for women inmates. The increased recognition of character and faith-based programs is only one paradigm in the development of faith-based programming and services for individuals in prison. Within the realm of the criminal justice system is the belief that faith-based organizations and communities frequently take charge in providing character and faith-building programs in prison for inmates to facilitate restoration and successful reintegration.

Eighty-five percent of the prison's faith-based spirituality in-prison programs across the country associate with Christianity. It is interesting to note that Jewish, Islamic, Buddhist, and inter/multi-faith religious programs while "spiritual-based" are not associated with the traditional faith of Christianity. These programs and non-Christian programs are not readily identifiable as faith-based programs.

Faith-Based Spirituality in Prison

Accordingly, there is a historical connection between longevity between the spheres of religion, penal policy, and criminal justice formation. The ideology of worship and correction has moved forward from the medieval period. Although the Western criminal justice system aim was to separate religious authorities and concepts, earlier religion culture remained.

One of the central assertions of fundamentalism is that "individuals are personally and morally responsible for their behavior, particularly deviance and misdeed. The criminology school of thought aligned with this statement. Such an assertion is "contrary to positivist theories that stressed situational and environmental factors beyond the immediate control of the individual. From the fundamentalist views, criminals have no excuse and should be held personally and fully responsible for their actions.

Religious belief plays a vital role in shaping the practice of punishment. The process by which religion influenced the correctional attitude is still undetermined. Religious beliefs that reflect compassionate expressions are predictive of support for restoration and rehabilitation. Religion has a positive association with attitudes that are more punitive and the compassionate side of religion. Forgiveness and faith share an association with decreased punitive approach and support for restoration and rehabilitation.

The impact of religiosity/spirituality on crime, recidivism, and compassionate attitudes toward women criminals demanded a lot more interest from the criminal justice system policy makers as it relates to funding, and the administration of public safety when developing programming. Emphasis must be placed on the direct measurement of individual religious/spiritual belief, value, and experience as the primary predictors of criminal behavior and the associated recidivism. A spiritual and mystical quest may offer a unique lifestyle change in the psyche, social ability, and life meaning among incarcerated women.

Interestingly, humanistic psychology characterized the approach to spirituality as the human personality. Thereby, opening the spiritual realm to the metaphorical river of the human nature, if understood, may lead to a world of mystical opportunities. Any rehabilitation or intervention that lends an opportunity for the deeper areas of the human psyche may ultimately come to the threshold of an individual's spiritual realm and lead service providers to be able to understand better that human personality and spirituality exist on the same continuum. If we are successful, this will move a vulnerable population such as incarcerated women from destructive personality characteristics to self-awareness, personal values, and socially acceptable behaviors.

Humanistic psychology has provided an arena for deliberations on spirituality for more than 40 years. In theory, the soul is the deepest core of our spiritual life; the sacred is a power that can nourish our souls. Spirituality is the result of having our heart freed of bitter experiences. Here in Hawai`i, this sacredness is the "Aina" (the land). The role of spirituality is evident amongst some incarcerated women. Spirituality is likely to influence change in criminal thinking and behavior. There is also the likelihood of possibly decrease the rates of recidivism. Spirituality with such great potential of restoring, rehabilitating and transforming, maladapted behaviors demands the call to action of our nation which are the founding spiritual principles of our country.

A focus on spiritual constructs for addressing the spiritual dimension makes it possible to create restoration and rehabilitation programs for incarcerated women to transform their lives and alter their criminal careers. Here are at least five such constructs that we know about prison faith-based programs.

1. At least 18 states and the federal government used some in-house faith-based program geared toward rehabilitating inmates. There were program offered classes such as anger management, substance abuse, ethical decision-making, and victim restitution based on religious or spiritual principles.
2. Faith-based programs that were explicitly motivated by specific religious principles run the risk of having difficulties based on the grounds of the Establishment Clause. However, many programs do exist which are explicitly motivated by Christian and Biblical principles. Programs that were interfaith or less defined by religious affiliation were less vulnerable to the Establishment Clause.
3. Faith-based programs continue to be useful as potential

interventions for reform, primarily for seeing improvement in prison discipline and reducing rates of recidivism.

4. We should be aware that most of the empirical studies on the effectiveness of such prisons are under clouds of severe methodological problems, which indicated little or no positive effectiveness in the use of faith-based programs.

5. The few empirical studies which have shown methodological soundness have failed to mention that faith-based programs reduced the rate of recidivism. The studies provided weak evidence for faith-based programs.

Gender-Responsive Rehabilitation

While risk factors for women are different from the risk factors of men, female offenders needs are often overlooked. The programs develop for male are offered to women offenders. These male designed programs inadequate. The application of single-gender focused programs can reduce the impact that rehabilitation has on female offenders as they differ from men in several ways. The ideology of risk, need, and responsivity have been established as a need of intervention for women offenders; however, the development and implementation of the philosophy for gender responsivity programs is still considered to be lacking.

Incarcerated women and the risk factors associated with female criminals are not well understood by behavioral scientists, policymakers, and society. Relatively little theory or empirical research has focused on women criminals or their need for gender-responsive rehabilitation programming. Little is known regarding the value of a service delivery that incorporates a woman's spirituality. Among the traditional gender-neutral theories, the indication is that women are ignored and that the explanation for offending is generalized across genders without any real empirical support.

Crimes committed by females are likely to be thought of as nonviolent crimes and based on financial needs of the offender. They are often believed to be drug related and powerless crimes. The majority of incarcerated women are from backgrounds that embrace violence against women, addiction, poverty, low self-esteem, or low self-efficacy. There is also the likelihood that women have been the primary caretakers of young children before their arrest. When compared to male criminals, incarcerated women criminals have a very different pathway. There are various risk factors associated with their presentation in the criminal justice system. There is a need for innovated ways of mitigating these issues.

House of Healing

Faith-based programs are active in the prison's facilities for the benefit of inmates. The programs have had some positive influence according to a few of the women. Programs which are gender-responsive take a holistic approach and are restorative in nature. The House of Healing program for grieving female prisoners described in *House of Healing: A Guide to Inner Power and Freedom*, addresses the psychosocial and the spiritual dimensions. The female offender is placed within the context of her relationships with others, the environment, community, and the criminal justice system. The program targeted issues such as (a) meditation, (b) stress management, and (c) cognitive reframing. Other issues focused included beneficial ways to transform anger; unhealthy guilt, resentment, and shame to encourage awareness of detrimental emotional responses and acquired behavior. Women were afforded the opportunity to explore beliefs and values, as well as their life journey from childhood to prison and the impact of a lifetime of loss and silenced grief.

Moving Away from Criminal Behavior

Many of the women who re-offended blamed themselves for poor decision-making and society appears to agree with the women's assessment for returning to prison. The focus on the development of a restoration and rehabilitation program needs to be holistic to include spirituality relations, beliefs, values, and personal meaning that will strengthen the internal character building attributes of incarcerated women. Such program will also contribute to better positioning the female offender for a successful transition and reentry to her community.

Reentry programs and policies must start with the restoration of mind, body, and soul for rehabilitation of incarcerated women. Application developers must take into consideration all areas of capabilities among female inmates to promote effective sustained reentry of the inmates back to their communities and to reduce the rates of recidivism.

Factors associated with becoming involved with the criminal justice system and processes associated with distancing a criminal lifestyle are yet to be given serious investigation. One such "hook" for women offenders is finding comfort in religion and spirituality to mitigate past victimization and to end their criminal lifestyles. The transcribed interviews revealed that some women criminals search for spiritual deliverance for making changes in their criminal lifestyle from committing a crime to improved relationships, increased self-awareness, self-esteem and self-efficacy, and improved decision-making.

This book provides educational information on the possibilities of filling a knowledge gap and bringing awareness to criminal justice practitioners, correctional administrators, policymakers, and professionals concerning restoration and rehabilitation programs for female and perhaps male offenders. The use of spirituality as a specific hook in prison programs' development could effectively improve life meaning and purpose, and could also reduce rates of recidivism among incarcerated women. Spirituality may provide additional strategies for mitigating risk factors linked to increased criminal activities such as positive relationships and improved self-esteem. In efforts to provide effective gender-responsive restoration and rehabilitation programs for incarcerated women and to reduce recidivism, the criminal justice administrators, correctional staff, faith-based practitioners, and professionals must encourage hope and faith for a healthier future for these women.

Criminal justice administrators, correctional officials, faith-based practitioners, and professionals have to engage in strategies to rehabilitate women offenders that decrease recidivism. The criminal justice leaders and policy makers need to understand the psyche of these women to create policies, procedures, and programs. Likewise, authorities must address the exclusive experiences, risk factors, pathways, and needs of incarcerated women, while providing for and advancing a platform for faith-based spirituality in women's correctional programming.

Correctional facilities procedures such as strip searches and confrontational practices used with male offenders have the potential of leaving women offenders traumatized and challenged in making behavioral changes. Rehabilitative policies and practices that are male-orientated are not effective in stopping the recidivism of incarcerated women. Women criminals need rehabilitative programs which address the risk factors that led to their incarceration. The need for programs that have potential to help women transition to lives free of crime should be the guiding principle for rehabilitating and reducing recidivism among women.

Summary

In summary, I suggest that faith-based correctional programs are useful in restoring, rehabilitating, and transforming women offenders and reducing recidivism. It is worth emphasizing the need to invest resources that support providers that would commit their lives servicing this underserved population. How can a society go wrong working to attaching meaning to the lived experiences of women offenders as it relates to self (body), mental (mind), and spiritual worthiness?

In addressing dysfunctional characteristics, being confronted with spirituality can transform a person's negative thinking, behavior, and attitude to positive behaviors and attitudes. It is clear that inmates who participate in faith-based spirituality programming have built reliance and perseverance characteristics. These two characteristics are qualities that move the inmates toward a transformational journey of a lifestyle which embraces behaviors that are visible and of value for a life free of crime. The significance of this communication adds to previous and current discussions on incarcerated women's restoration, transformation, and rehabilitation strategies.

My book has the potential to advance the knowledge in the field of psychological and faith-based spirituality programming for meeting the complex needs in restoring, rehabilitating, and transforming incarcerated women while reducing rates of relapse and recidivism. Through the use of faith-based spirituality, as well as identifying the gaps for future discussion and educational opportunities the next few chapters will provide valuable insight.

SECTION THREE

Dialog with Incarcerated Women

The purpose of this section is to share the dialog of a group of incarcerated women here in Hawai`i's Women's Community Correctional Facility. Here you are presented with what came from the personal interviews with the female inmates. Of course, the discussion focus is in the interest of learning about the lived experiences, perceptions, and meanings of faith-based spirituality among incarcerated women in Hawai`i. The broader discussion was to capture the definition of spirituality among the incarcerated women in Hawai`i. Two subtopic questions also guided the inquiry: (a) What are the lived experiences of incarcerated women in Hawai`i regarding spirituality? And (b) What are the lived experiences of incarcerated women in Hawai`i relating to the role of spirituality in their rehabilitation?

By spending time and sharing with these inmates, I was able to identify the spiritual experiences in this population and gained some insight regarding ways to develop gender-responsive rehabilitation programs suited for incarcerated women. This book is written based on the findings with suggestions that may be useful in reducing the rate of recidivism among female inmates in Hawai`i.

Population of Women

There were 20 slots for potential women to participate in the in-prison, faith-based Total Life Recovery (TLR) program at the Women's Community Correction Center in Hawai`i. However, five of the potential inmates were no longer available for participation in the discussion on the subject of faith-based spirituality among incarcerated women in Hawai`i. Fifteen inmates who currently attended the Total Life Recovery (TLR) program at Women's Community Correction Center in Hawaii engaged in the discussion for my book.

The purpose of the book was explained in detail in a group setting. Informed Consent forms were signed and collected from the inmates. Prisoners were given a copy of their signed consent form as the intention is to publish the book. Inmates were excited and honored to participate in the discussion and the development of the book. Demographic information was collected using a 19-item screening instrument developed primarily for the book. Face to face interviews was also guided by another 15-item interview questionnaire which ensured that all inmates were asked the same questions.

Women's Demographics

The ethnic background of the participants was as follows: 2=Hawaiian, 7=Part-Hawaiian with a mixture of Filipino, Japanese, and Caucasian, 1=African American, 1= Alaskan Indian, 1= Asian, 1= Black/White, 1=Pacific Islander and 1=Samoan. Thirteen women reported having at least one or more children. Two women reported having no children. The levels of education reported among the inmates were seven high school graduates, and three with at least two years of college. One woman completed four years of college. Four participants dropped out of school. Tables 1 and 2, and Figures 1 and 2 present a distribution of the demographics related to the inmates.

All the detainees in the book considered themselves spiritual, and they participate in a faith-based program, know of God/Spirituality, or attended church before incarceration. The religious distribution or spirituality affiliation among these women consist of 14 inmates claiming a label as being Christians and one identified as Seventh Day Adventist. The status of the women was as follows: six divorced, two separated, six single, and three married as shown in Table 1.

Table 1
Marital status of inmates

Marital Status Distribution				
	Single	Married	Separated	Divorced
15 Inmates	6	3	4	2

The age criteria for the inmates are between the ages of 21 and 71 (see below).

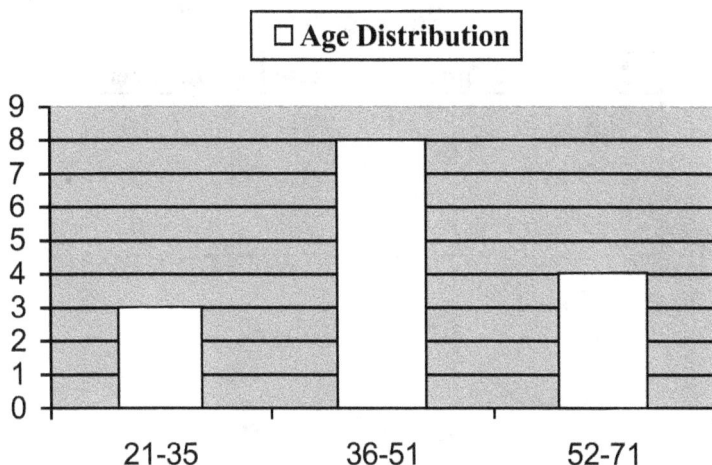

Figure 1: Age Grouping of inmates interviewed for this book.

Additional information gathered about these inmates included the number of arrests and the number of incarcerations that they have experienced. Eight of the women shared that they were arrested one or two times. Five mentioned being arrested from three times up to six times. Two other women reported having been arrested at least seven times or more as shown in Table 2. Nine of the women said that while they have been detained on several occasions, this was their first incarceration. One woman stated that this incarceration was her second incarceration. Three other women reported being incarcerated on three other occasions. The last two inmates said that this was their fifth time being in incarceration at this prison. The distribution of charges associated with the inmates are as follows: five inmates were incarcerated for a drug offense, three inmates have been accused of theft or burglary charges, and seven inmates were incarcerated for violent offenses as shown in Figure 2.

Table 2

Arrests and incarcerations of inmates

Self-reported		
Number of Times	Arrested	Incarcerated
1 to 2	8	10
3 to 6	5	5
7 and Over	2	0

Note: 15 Inmates

Crime Distribution

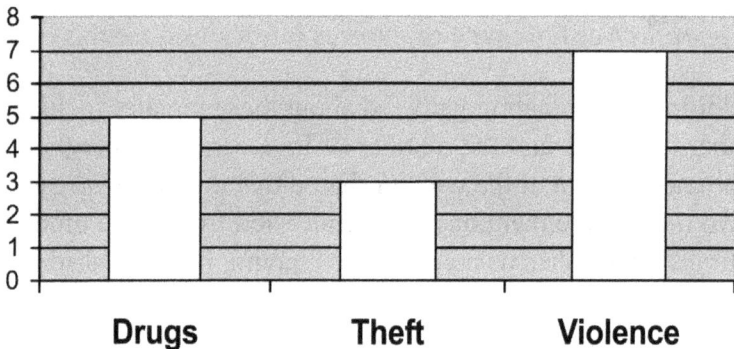

Figure 2: Crime distribution grouping of inmates

Collection of Interviews

The protocol for the interviews in this book is based on the discussion questions, the handling of the information handled, and the group of inmates. The way of collecting interviews was well within the lines of completing a phenomenological study. This method is also ideal for gaining an understanding of the lived experiences, perceptions, and worldviews of the inmate's experiences of the phenomenon (spirituality). A purposive group of 15 inmates was selected to provide interview feedback.

An additional protocol for collecting the interviews for the book included several instruments, such as (a) a 19-item screening questionnaire, (b) interviews, and (c) digital audio recordings. The 19-item screening questionnaire contained demographic information. Recorded interviews were used to collect verbatim statements from the inmates for clustering like-schemas. An initial group session was held at the prison. The women signed informed consents during this session. The screening questionnaire was handed out to all inmates willing to take part in the book project. The nature of qualitative sampling is convenient and purposive which is the classification of how the offenders were selected. All fifteen inmates, who participated in the in-prison, faith-based program participated. This approach to sampling was appropriate for the phenomenon under discussion and the questions for which answers were being sought.

In-depth, face-to-face audiotape interviews were scheduled for the 15 inmates participating in the book. Audio recordings are kept strictly confidential. During the interviews, inmates were given an F-number (F1-15) to protect privacy and confidentiality. Interviews were held in a semi-private space. Inmates agreed not to discuss the types of questions or their conversation with anyone. Fifteen interview questions guided the stories the inmates told regarding their lived experiences and the role of spirituality in their rehabilitation plans.

The collection process was complicated due to repeated interruptions during the interviews. The meeting room was not very private. Privacy was invaded several times, resulting in having to stop the interview process when prison official needed the room. Technical difficulties arose when metal doors were slammed, and sounds from the air conditioner vents reverberating. The concrete wall echoed and distorted the audio recordings. These challenges are taken into consideration in the transcriptions of muffled sounds and an inability to transcribe some of the interviews from some parts of the audio recordings.

Saturation was reached among the 15 inmates as no new themes emerged in the interviews. The 15 inmates were sufficient in reaching saturation. The information collected during the interviews was transcribed, and themes or units of meanings were clustered and analyzed. The transcription of each interview was taken from the digital audio recordings verbatim and captured in a data table for each respondent to each question.

In the final group session with the inmates, each inmate received a transcription set in a table that detailed the women's responses. Inmates were asked to review the transcribed interview for accuracy and validation of their responses, opinions, and perspectives. Written consent to ensure protection and integrity of the information are retained from participants. The inmates granted permission for the safeguard and protection of the digital audio recordings to me. The original records are owned by the interviewing facilitator and are securely stored for five years.

Analysis of the Reviews

A qualitative method of a phenomenological design is best for adding meaning to this topic. A phenomenological design is employed to describe and make sense of particular phenomenon under discussion, rather than to develop a theoretical model associated with grounded theory. Phenomenological communication analysis is used to organize and analyze the inmates' responses.

The approach to understanding the information included the process of epoche. The epoche process is used to enhance the rigorous systematic procedures and to set aside biases and judgments. The focus is on the perceptions of the inmates' views of the phenomenon. Taking no position, not using foreknowledge, and being nonjudgmental add credibility to the investigation. The meaning units emerged from the interviews. Some were single words, and some were statements or groups of words. This process enabled awareness to be given to the phenomenon precisely as inmates presented, without additions or deletion.

Search for Essence

The interviews yielded hundreds of topics. The topics were closely related among all the women. Twenty-three statements were carefully examined and bracketed to form essential clusters according to emerged themes or meaning units. In this phenomenological process, we seek to find and understand the essence of the phenomenon (spirituality) by using a method called free imaginative variation. The free imagination variation method rests largely upon the ability to stimulate possibilities. Whatever was given became one example of a possible instance of the phenomenon, and other opportunities were encouraged by multiplication of options.

Provided are descriptions from the thematic analysis of what was experienced in the textual descriptions. Further meanings were considered from the roles, functions, and different perspectives or imaginative variations, which helped to form the foundational structure of the phenomenon. The data analysis revealed results of four essential themes. Theme descriptions are presented in a textual structure description of the inmates' meanings and essences of their experiences.

The relevant statements were peer reviewed to confirm the accuracy of the originally transcribed interviews, the meaning units, and the common themes. The results are presented using the four common themes of the inmates' descriptions. The inmates were willing and openly shared views about their spirituality, growth, and desire to never come back to prison.

Finally, the composite summary of descriptions of the phenomenon was developed through the synthesis of the structural and textual descriptions of the inmates' experiences. Coding and clustering led to 23 meaning units which resulted in bracketing and distilling the meaning units. These processes produced the four emerging themes. These common themes became the essential, invariant structure of ultimate "essence" which was in the voices of the women inmates and captured the meaning ascribed to their faith-based spiritual lived experience.

SECTION FOUR

Results of Interview Analysis

Authentication of the reality of spirituality lies in the first-person perceptions of the life experiences of the women inmates. The information analysis process led to the identification of four essential themes that captured the collective textual and structural descriptions of the essence of the perceptions, opinions, beliefs, and lived spiritual experiences of the phenomenon of spirituality among incarcerated women in Hawai`i.

All the inmates identified themselves as being spiritual and participated in the prison's faith-based Total Life Recovery program (TLR). The 15 inmate's responses on essential points formed the basis for discussions, recommendations, and the book's outcome. Based on bracketing and eliminating similar, unrelated, repetitive and overlapping words and statements, the full transcriptions of all the inmates' responses were not included in this document. Responses from inmates are represented in quotations. The analysis coded and categorized 23 meaning units that formed the four major themes. The conceptualization of having a relationship, the lack of a relationship, learning to change, and being transformed emerged clearly throughout the interviewing, coding, and bracketing processes. The four major common themes are the following:

1. 1.   The perception of Spirituality as a relationship.
2. 2.   The lack of a relationship with God.
3. 3.   The desire to change attitudes and behaviors.
4. 4.   A transformation of the heart (soul) and mind.

Textual-Structure Descriptions

Theme 1: The Perception of Spirituality as a Relationship

Incarcerated women in this book identify spirituality as a relational phenomenon. One of the themes that emerged from the women inmates was the importance of having a relationship with God. The majority of the women believed that the Bible, the Word of God, gives rules and direction for a spiritual way of life. The inmates felt that relationships with God, Jesus, Holy Spirit, Lord, the Bible, Christ, the invisible driving force, and the land have afforded them freedom, positive change, and commitment to live accountable and responsible lives.

Much more emphasis was placed on being in or having a relationship rather than on religion. When prompted with the question, "What is spirituality to you?" one inmate stated, "I love God with all my heart and am giving myself all to him." Another inmate said, "I know God and about letting him interact with your life." Another inmate stated, "I had a relationship with the Lord. There were things that I neglected in the past. Now I reflect on what God had done in my life before incarceration, oh how I fail the Lord. There are times I obey and times I don't care because to my self-centeredness. I had lots of warnings. My mind was not founded in God."

When prompted with the question, "What is spirituality to you?" three other inmates provided textual descriptions of a relationship as the essence of their lived experience in giving meaning to spirituality and stated, "a relation first with Christ and then with others." Another said, "A relationship between human flesh spirit and faith-based spirit. The Holy Spirit is still in my heart. I believe that we do have a God. Spirituality is what I do for others." One of the inmate's textual descriptions spoke solely to a relationship of all aspects of her life. She described her lived experienced in the way she lived out spirituality every day. The inmate stated that "Spirituality is what I live through each day, my belief and what I carry with me. It is how you live your life. Spirituality is the spirit with you. My belief, my religion, my way of living, my acts, and everything I do would be my spirituality. I experienced spirituality when I feel much more peace, assurance, and revelation." Each of the 15 inmates described her essence of the meaning of spirituality as the ultimate relationship with a variation of a divine invisible being. As a delineation from most of the inmates, one of the 15 inmates provided textual descriptions as a connection to culture.

The phenomenon of spirituality is hard to define and was evident in the variation among the women's stories of a relationship and connection. All the inmates' responses started with the words link to and as each interview developed all the inmates were using the Word of God. The relationship was bound to a higher conscious, an invisible driving force, and a power greater than one's self which included the land.

When asked the question, "What is spirituality to you?" one of the inmates stated, "Spirituality is connected to a higher conscious, it is innate higher, pre info can see a spiritual freedom. It is awe like childbirth a powerful experience with joy." Another inmate said, "An invisible driving force and faith of that of something invisible." Another inmate described spirituality as "knowing and not being of this world. There is nothing to compare personally or culturally. It feels better than anything; it is hard to explain, there's nothing that could compare." Another inmate said, "Spirituality is a connection to a higher power, goodness, and the essence of who I am." One inmate relationship was prevalent to culture and stated, "Spirituality is a power greater than me that filled with inner peace that aligns me a spiritual foundation that comes from God. I feel my spirituality by giving back to the land, rain, plants and taking responsibility to care for and about these things. Love of the land, it will give back to you in produce. I have a personal relationship. Most of my spiritual experiences come from my culture."

Theme 2: The Lack of a Relationship with God

Another theme that emerged during the interviews was learning to change. Many of the inmates believed that it was paramount to regulate their emotions, change their heart and soul, their thinking, and behavior to stay out of trouble and out of prison. The inmates in this book ascribed their criminal behavior patterns to not having a relationship with God, not knowing God, and not serving God before incarceration. One inmate highlighted that she had been to a lot of programs, but this program offered the freedom to change. Another inmate stated, "learning about God and having more faith in God saved my life. I always wanted to have instant gratification, but today, I have a purpose. I am learning to be dependent on God and not relying on people."

When asked, "What was spirituality like for you before incarceration?" four of the 15 women inmates reported not knowing God. For example, an inmate stated, "It sounds strange to believe in God." Another inmate said, "I didn't have any spirituality." Another inmate said, "I don't think that I had anything spiritual.... Uh no knowledge of what spiritual was." One inmate shared: "uh my spirituality when I was out there uh, I did not have any. I didn't serve him (God). I had no fellowship."

Some inmates believe that other individuals negatively influenced their desire to serve God, as well as their self-centeredness and desire for instant gratification which stood between them and their ability to have a servant relationship with God and others. Another four out of 15 inmates, when asked, "What was spirituality like for you before incarceration?" reported that they knew of God and had some relationship, but did not serve or interact with God before incarceration. For example, one inmate stated, "I knew of God, heard about him, and never took the time to let him interact in my life." Another inmate said, "I knew God; I threw my life into my work. I stopped asking and thanking God." Another inmate stated, "I knew God from what I saw from my grand aunts; it caused me not to want to have anything to do with church or anything related to God." Another inmate stated, "Knew God and being about letting him intervene in my life;" she also said, "I never allowed God in."

Learning to change their attitudes and behavior for these inmates was described from the perception of "not wanting to hurt anyone anymore including herself." Each inmate contributed her learning to change to the teaching, classes, and counseling of the Total Life Recovery (TLR), two-year faith-based, in-prison program. The TLR program was described by the inmates as a heart changing and mind altering experience. The inmates believed that other programs and treatments only dealt with the cognitive aspect of their brokenness and not the broken matters of the heart and soul.

The women shared some experiences of having been traumatized before incarceration. The inmates expressed feelings of having been stripped of hope, everything, betrayed, hurt, went in and out of prison with the same mentality, and were without hope, filled with shame, guilt, and resentment. Inmates highlighted what they perceived as the roots of where their lives would have to change.

Theme 3: The Desire to Change Attitudes and Behaviors

The inmates believed that their incarceration was divine intervention. The inmates reported feeling that being incarcerated put them in a safe environment, a situation where God could get their attention. The inmates described this period in their life as a time to be still, quiet the spirit and mind, and a time to get in touch with their purpose in life. As the women entered the TLR program to begin their journey, inmates reported using the Bible, the Word of God, for application in discovering the underlying foundation of a spiritual walk. One inmate highlighted how TLR approach to spirituality has worked in her life: "I feel that I have a chance to learn about God. TLR teaches me – life work with God. It easier to work with God instead of running away - helps me to understand that everything about my work that I do in my life revolves around God."

Learning to take this spiritual walk according to the inmates started with the Bible, the Word of God, referred to by most inmates as The Word. Reading the Bible, completing the Genesis course and other classes address false beliefs and thinking errors and aid these women in recovering from compulsive and addictive behavior while supporting strategies for self-worth and integrity. The inmates stated they learned among other things to have faith, trust, hope, and accountability to God and others. For example, one inmate when asked, "What is the role of spirituality in your rehabilitation?" stated, "It is a positive, purposeful changing force. God has a plan for my life. Godly/spiritual is a desire to live differently. Empower me with the word of God and encourage me to look in the upward direction. Gives the opportunity to heal and love to be committed and consistent. I want positive change. As for me, I love my creator. I decided that I did not want to

hurt anyone else anymore. I needed to learn, and I wanted to learn."
When asked, "What is the role of spirituality in your rehabilitation?"
another inmate said, "It helps me to come closer to the person that I
have faith in which is God. We don't just learn. It makes me open.
I'm actually happy and content. I learned to be verbal. There is a lot
of things I know; it makes me see what can be done in a person life.
I want to change my mind and my heart."

One other inmate when asked, "What is the role of spirituality in
your rehabilitation?" stated, "Come to the meat of the word connection
to correction for turning our life around. Total Life Recovery gave
me back my life. I can use my testimony to help others."

Many of the responses were repetitive with the reply of another
inmate who stated, that "Spirituality is contributed to coming to
know Jesus, God, and more better spiritual principles, to be of service
to God and others. I have gained head and heart knowledge. To be
connected with the church. God can use me."

Theme 4: A Transformation of the Heart (Soul) and Mind

A conversion was another theme that emerged from the interviews
as a life changing factor. Most of the inmates expressed feelings
of having a desire and choice to change. The inmates believed that
dealing with the core issues have provided them freedom from the
valley and trauma and shame and guilt. All of the inmates felt that
TLR has helped in transforming their lives from a life of criminal
thinking and behavior to a productive and purposive life in service
to others, and acceptance of a way of living based on accountability
and responsibility. One inmate shared, "I cannot be the person that I
walked into prison. I have confidence and drive that let me know that
I can accomplish something. It is more of a life changing opportunity
in building our spiritual path." Another inmate said, "Doesn't want
that life anymore. Every seed has a consequence. It is my choice to
make the right decision. God has plans that I'll follow when I get
support, stay involved, and connected."

Many inmates believed that being transformed spiritually was the
role of the teaching and spirituality components of the TLR program.

Inmates highlighted the importance of spirituality concerning changing the heart and renewing of the mind.

One inmate stated, "TLR is like having a moral compass inside of you. It helps strengthen that voice inside of me where I developed reasonable responses. A sense of worth, love me and others." Another inmate said, TLR has helped me to know and understand the Bible, the truth, and to be real about myself. To break down walls, expose secrets, and makes me feel that I belong, has self-worth, and is worthy as a child of God. It helps me to be a woman of excellence. When asked, "What is the role of spirituality in your rehabilitation?" another inmate stated, "It has given me a lot of corrections, responsibilities, and accountability for a new life without crime. A new life with Jesus, I found peace, serenity, restoration. I know how to deal with situations today and how to be accountable for my actions." Another inmate said, "TLR has helped me with discipline, obedience, respect, humility, forgiveness, restoration, emotional/mental healing, acceptance, exposure, love and integrity--, um yeah self-worth, potential endless use of my voice, confidence to be an encouragement to self and others. I am somebody – God has a plan and purpose with hope for me. I cannot be disappointed in life. I feel empowered as a woman through God's grace and mercy."

Summary

The primary purpose of this research was to explore the importance of faith-based spirituality among women in Hawai`i who are incarcerated, make a contribution to research exploring how faith-based programs can affect behavior, and possibly reduce recidivism among female criminals. Later in chapter five, there will be a composite summary of descriptions of the phenomenon (spirituality) through the synthesis of the textual and structural descriptions of the experiences of 15 inmates from face-to-face audio recorded interviews.

Further handling of the audio recorded interviews was to transcribe and verify the inmates given information and have professional peers who work in the field to review the information. Epoche was helpful in allowing the author to set aside biases. Bracketing, coding, and categorizing reduced the information to four common themes. These terms are relevant to and are best known by qualitative researchers.

The results of the information examination provide four common themes, (a) the perception of spirituality as a relationship, (b) the lack of a relationship with God, (c) the desire to change attitudes and behaviors, and (d) a transformation of the heart (soul) and mind. The results indicate that all 15 women inmates believe that spirituality and the role of spirituality in their rehabilitation were relational driven. They also believed that spirituality was essential for their recovery. The fifteen perspectives involved a relationship with divine individuals or forces, as well as learning their life's meaning and purpose, serving others, and being committed and consistent in an outward direction of praising, worshipping, and following God's laws for maximum change in their lives.

Results from this book may help in understanding the lived experiences of spirituality among incarcerated women and impact the recognition of spirituality as a change agent in restoration and rehabilitation of incarcerated women. The information and knowledge provided also offer opportunities for consideration in the development of gender-responsive programs and treatment of inmates. Application developers, administrators, and policymakers can also gain a better insight of the role of spirituality in the lived experiences of the prisoners inside of Hawai`i prison walls. Furthermore, section five will present recommendations and implications for practice, limitations, and directions for future discussions on spirituality and inmates inside Hawai`i prison walls.

SECTION FIVE

Discussions, Implications, and Recommendations

The purpose of this part of the book is to provide a conversation in an interpretation of the information resulting from the interviews. Also discussed in this chapter are limitations, implications for practice, and possible future discussions. At the end of this chapter are the recommendations for future investigation and a conclusion based on the information from the women interviewed.

This book produces several topics that possibly add to the existing literature and research on faith-based spirituality and incarcerated women. The information is distinctly and may be of interest to leaders working in the field of restoration and rehabilitation of female offenders. This book also provides an opportunity for the incarcerated women to share their lived spiritual experiences and the impact those experiences have had in their decision-making processes.

The purpose of this type of discussion allows one the opportunity of gaining an understanding and insight into the lived experiences of incarcerated woman through her personal worldview. The goal of this review is to explore ways to integrate the meanings of spirituality assigned by the women into their restoration, rehabilitation, and transformation. Also, allowing for inquiring about the lived experiences of incarcerated women in Hawai`i regarding their world view of spirituality. Furthermore, these kinds of discussions assist in helping the services providers and public safety in understanding the lived experiences of women prisons in Hawai`i as it relates to the role of spirituality in their restoration and rehabilitation?

Discussion about the Contributors

Fifteen women inmates purposively recruited from the Total Life Recovery program at the Women's Community Correctional Center in Hawai`i participated in the book. Saturation was reached quickly as the interviewees provided no new information. Four common themes emerged from data analysis regarding spiritual beliefs among the selected women. The themes appear to have influenced the women in several ways. Some had a desire to change and improve their behavior as it affected their families. Others began to focus on how to become a better citizen in their community. Some were concerned with making changes to become more accountable to society. The information analysis coded and categorized 23 different units, which are divided among the four overarching themes:

1. The perception of Spirituality as a relationship.
2. The lack of a relationship with God.
3. The desire to change attitudes and behaviors.
4. A transformation of the heart and mind (soul).

Support for Elkins belief that the soul is the home of one's spiritual belief system came forth. The expectations appear to nourish the soul and influence behaviors based on experiences of relationships in the invisible realm. The information in this book is grounded in the theoretical framework of the relational theory of Altman & Taylor, 1973and Covington & Bloom, 2006. One's moral code may motivate one to avoid criminal activity. The theoretical framework illuminated how a person's moral code of conduct may erode or decline. The moral code of conduct could then influence individuals to indulge in immoral or criminal behavior. The results show that when the inmates made a choice to seek spiritual fulfillment or spiritual guidance, they were able to make changes in the way they perceived and treated themselves, others, and the larger community. The following section provided a discussion of the four common themes.

Discussion of Common Themes

The perception of spirituality as a relationship.

Inmates conveyed to the researcher their belief that the Bible is the Word of God, which influenced their decision to turn to God or a higher power. The Word of God, in turns, allowed them to have hope and to receive healing from their internal wounds. Hope is a gift given to individuals from God. Hope may act as an anchor to steady the heart or soul. Ideally, it is not based on emotions but the unchanging words and promises found in the Bible.

Eight of the women inmates described spirituality as a relationship and seven defined spirituality as a connection. Inmates described the relationship as an interaction between themselves and a powerful supernatural driving force. Different names were used when referring to the power source. Names such as Jesus, God, Holy Spirit, my Creator, Lord, and my higher power, were interchangeable.

According to the inmates, the divine relationship was one of unconditional and unfailing love and forgiveness. Inmates believed that certain Bible verses must be taken literally. One example used by several women is found in the gospel of John. "For God so loved the world that he gave His one and only Son, that whoever believes in him shall not perish but have eternal life" (John 3:16 NIV).

One inmate stated, "Spirituality to me is an invisible force within my body. It is called the Holy Spirit due to the blood of Jesus who died for us on the cross." Another inmate said, "Spirituality is my relationship, knowing and understanding who you are serving. Open yourself to be led by the Holy Spirit to become Christ-like."

Another inmate said, Spirituality to me is a relationship with God. It is making a commitment to live according to the Bible and what it teaches me. A spiritual component... Ways to prevent the return to prison......um Things start falling in place......um God is the connection between the cognitive and behavior.

The inmates expressed the need to build spiritual relationships by:

- Reading and understanding the Bible
- Believing and acting on the Word of God
- Praying and trusting God
- Asking for direction and guidance
- Praising and worshiping God
- Fellowshipping with others seeking a spiritual relationship
- Attending Genesis (Bible based self-help therapy)
- Group-classes' like Celebrate Recovery
- Inmates appeared to see themselves differently once they believed that they had or were involved in a personal relationship

with God (Jesus, Higher Power, Holy Spirit, Lord).

According to Lederman (2008), "For our sake God made Christ to be a sinless sacrifice, who knew no sin so that in and through Christ we might become...the righteousness of God" [what we ought to be, approved and acceptable and in right relationship with Him, by His goodness] (p. 264).

The lack of relationship with God

A lack of a relationship with a spiritual and mystical being appeared to be a major factor that encouraged poor decision-making and unacceptable behavioral practices including criminal acts. Based on the Inmates' responses when asked, what was spirituality like before incarceration? They believed that they were lost, without direction, and driven by self-will. The inmates indicated that the lack of a relationship with a spiritual or higher power was a major factor that encouraged poor decision-making and unacceptable behavioral practices including criminal acts.

According to the inmates, lack of a spiritual relationship led them to feel confused about God and spiritual and moral or ethical issues. The inmates felt unable to have intimacy in their relationships (both human and divine). Research indicated that when inmates felt they had no connection with God, they experienced feelings of isolation. They used the words: lost, without spiritual connection, lacking fellowship, void of kindness or caring for others, and a distorted view of the world. One inmate stated, "I was lost with a lot of spirituality. I did not know how to live spiritual. It sounds really strange to believe in God or to have a relationship with anyone except me, myself, and I." Another inmate said, "I would go to church after my second time in prison. God was an avenue that gave me a chance to get out of prison. I was angry and hurt. I did not have a relationship with God, but I always believed in God. I did not live as I believed."

Another inmate stated, "The event that made spirituality meaningful to me was being stripped of everything. I had no hope. I did not value family, education, or friends." Another inmate said incarceration influenced my spirituality. When you get here, you are stripped, torn. Everything was taken away. I do not know how people make it without hope. I had no reasons to do well. I have to have a life meaning other than incarceration, and this life is meaningless. According to Van Voorhis et al., (2010) risk factors for women offenders includes troubled relationships, poverty, health disparity, the need for improved self-esteem, and self-efficacy. When improved, these variables seem to be critical factors for reducing recidivism.

The desire to change attitudes and behaviors

Another theme that emerged was the desire to be changed. The inmates did not want to leave prison in the same state which they arrived. The women wanted somehow to become "women of excellence." They used this phrase in the written philosophy of the Total Life Recovery program, which the inmates recited daily. As quoted: We were once on the outside looking in. We no longer want to stay hidden in the shadows. Although our spirits have been wounded, we will not be defeated! Our hearts have a burning desire to change. A flame of hope has been ignited from within. We can lean on our sisters for support, together overcoming obstacles. We will be able to clarify and resolve our issues when we walk away from worries and move toward joy. Leaving behind conflicts and moving toward resolution, giving up emptiness, we move towards fulfillment.

Society says to change the woman you must first change the behavior. God says to first change the heart of a woman then the behavior will change. God is changing our hearts and renewing our minds. We know through God's care, we are beginning a new course in life, and we'll be taking steps toward a beautiful future, as "Na Wahine O Kupono" women of excellence!

According to Nedderman (2008), to change in our spiritual growth, we must display maturity. For change to occur within an individual, three things must precipitate the desire to change. Individual must hurt enough to the point that there is no choice but to change. Individual must learn or believe sufficient to have the hope to change.

Individual must receive enough unconditional love to be motivated toward change.

Hope appears to be the hook for change that drives the desire for a relationship with God. In the Old Testament of the Bible, King David referred to hope when he instructed, "O Israel put your hope in the Lord, for with the Lord is unfailing love and with him is full redemption" (Psalm 130:7 NIV). The Apostle Paul stated in the New Testament, "May the God of hope fill you with all joy and peace as you trust in him, so that you may overflow with hope by the power of the Holy Spirit" (Romans 15:12-14 NIV). These two Scriptures are examples of positive affirmations throughout the Bible for building a relationship with God, being hopeful because of the love of God, and His qualities of faithfulness, grace, and goodness.

Changing the condition of the heart (soul) in a positive manner would result in cognitive changes in behaviors, values, and beliefs in the lives of incarcerated women in Hawai`i. Results in this book speak volumes to the needs and desires of the women who want to learn how to follow the Word of God in hope for change to become better individuals than they were before incarceration. Inmates expressed a desire to be more aware, more accountable, and more responsible as individuals. The inmates felt this change could occur if they could learn to have more faith and trust in God. All the inmates said that they wanted to get to be more humble and to develop self-control. The women noted that in order for change to occur, there must first be an admission that something was wrong and lacking in their lives.

The first act on the pathway to change was a confession. Entering the in-prison TLR program, the inmates began to form relationships with each other. Reportedly they began to realize they needed to change both their thinking and behavior. Through private, one-to-one counseling with volunteers that support the faith-based program, inmates are encouraged to pray for forgiveness of sin and salvation or a right relationship with God. In the session, a counselor may lead a prayer such as the Prayer of Salvation in Nedderman (2008),

> Lord, I have a sinful nature (to do and to think in the wrong manners), and I need you. I believe that Jesus is the Son of God that He died on the cross to save me and to forgive all my transgressions. Lord, I trust in You, and I asked that You

now come and take up permanent residence in my heart. Lord, stimulate my hope again, not in people and things or even in myself. Give me fresh hope in you and your Word. I ask you to anchor and establish my heart in your hope because You will never fail me. In Jesus name, Amen (p. 264)

Duvall et al. (2008) suggested that faith-based values such as faith, prayer, mindfulness, and hope might provide a psychological alternative to embracing abnormal criminality belief system that is often associated with dysfunctional behavior. One inmate stated I have been to many programs. This faith-based program offers the freedom to change. Spirituality is like reading the Bible, all the classes that I am taking, daily devotions, and attending Genesis therapy. I am learning to have more faith in God. Before the Total Life program, I would always want to instant gratification and lived day by day. I wanted to die. Incarceration and TLR saved my life. Today, I have a purpose. I am learning to be dependent on God and not relying on people.

A transformation of the heart (soul) and mind.

The final theme, which emerged from the information, is that of having a transformed life. Inmates believed that the condition of their hearts and minds needed to be transformed if they were going to stay out of prison. In the Bible it is written, "The fool says in his heart, "There is no God." "They are corrupt, and their ways are vile; no one does good" (Psalm 53:1, NIV).

All inmates believed that to become different individuals They need to deal with their heart issues of guilt, shame, and hurt. Inmates believe they are being transformed by the renewing of the mind and the changing their heart (soul). This belief has led to behavioral changes and a desire to improve even more. One inmate said, "With a relationship with God, faith, and going by the Bible rules, I became a new person."

The idea of behavior transformation in this book also dealt with the need to remove selfish attitudes to acquire a selflessness attitude. The role of spirituality among the inmates includes being consistent and dedicated to serving God and others. One inmate stated, "My purpose in life is to serve others."

Some researchers believe that a faith-based rehabilitation philosophy should include strategies for rehabilitative efforts and self-betterment efforts, which would offer encouragement to individual inmates. One inmate said, "My purpose is what God wants me to do opposed to what I want to do. I have a greater purpose than selling drugs." Other scholars have implied that spiritual beliefs reflecting compassionate expressions such as forgiveness and faith are predictive of support for rehabilitation and reducing recidivism.

Repeatedly stated by inmates was their desire to change which would be evidenced by remaining out of prison and living a life of meaning and purpose. The inmates realized that behavior patterns such as stealing, cheating, manipulating, lying, using alcohol and drugs, hurting others, unforgiving, bitterness, blaming others and society were not productive and were most destructive. The inmates felt their best option was a change in life purpose based on God's unconditional love and Biblical principles. Inmates believed that the role of spirituality offered an opportunity to be transformed through knowledge and understanding of God's Word, and by believing in and trusting in God. An often-quoted Scripture was Jeremiah (29:11, NIV) "For I know the plans I have for you," declares the Lord, "plans to prosper you and not to harm you, plans to give you hope and future."

One inmate stated, "For me to have a new life without crime, I found that I needed a new life with Jesus. I have been given peace, serenity, and restoration. I am dependent on Jesus. I know how to deal with situations today. I know how to be accountable for my actions." Another inmate stated, "I am somebody. God has a plan and a purpose of hope for me. I cannot be disappointed in life. Through God's grace and mercy, I feel empowered as a woman."

And another inmate said, "To know and to understand the truth of the Bible, is to be real about me. Um to break down walls, expose secrets and to build a strong foundation and a relationship with my Lord make me feel that I belong. Um... Self-worth, I am a worthy child of God. It helps me to be a woman of excellence. Spirituality has helped me to come to know Jesus.... um God more-better. I have gained spiritual principles um like being in service to God and others. I have gained head and heart knowledge and the opportunity to be connected to the church or where ever God can use me. My purpose is to be a part of God's family. I feel that I belong. I have self-worth. I am a worthy child of God. I am a woman of excellence."

Limitations

Although I based this book on the current research, the limitations that may lead to questioning the validity, generalizability, or the trustworthiness of the information in this book may be concerns with the size of the group, the Inmates' self-report, and personal integrity. The information may be generalized from the facilitator's perspective only to the population involved in the discussion.

A small group of 15 inmates in a faith-based program who are incarcerated in Hawai`i and the extensive research do give some generalization power to the discussion on faith-based spirituality among incarcerated women. The information may not be generalized to the entire women's prison population. The personal nature of the questions and desire to impress the facilitator may have caused the inmates to over or under report as it was related to social desirability. The inmates' self-report most likely influenced the value of the information, as an attempt to impress.

Clearly, during the interviews, the inmates wanted to answer each question with "The Total Life Recovery Program is an excellent program" or "I love this program." This was cause for a substantial amount of redirecting and refocusing inmates to the guided questions. Inmates' personal integrity (or lack thereof) affected the integrity of the information. Inmates' discussions were for the program and what they thought they needed to say about the program more so than about their lived spiritual experiences.

Implications for Practice

By documenting the perceptions, opinions, and worldviews on the impact of spirituality on the life of women inmates in Hawai`i, a potential strategy to seriously consider emerged for addressing the rehabilitation of women prisoners. Spirituality appears to be a single strategy that provides a holistic approach with practical implications in the development of gender-responsive in-prison programs for women offenders. Another implication for practice based on the results of this book is that women offenders may have a better chance for rehabilitation when provided a group environment that is sensitive and safe. The results also imply that there was a direct link between spirituality and moral behavior.

Inmates needed to process both sides of offenses. It is likely that inmates needed to confess to criminal thinking and behavior while being able to acknowledge the offenses committed against them. The criminal justice system may benefit by providing avenues for the voices of incarcerated women in Hawai`i to be heard in a sensitive and non-threatening setting.

The findings in this book may be of value in guiding policymakers, criminal justice practitioners, and professionals in developing future in prison, gender-responsive programming for incarcerated women of Hawai`i. It may also assist in addressing risk factors and other complex needs of women offenders where other rehabilitation efforts have not been affected, such as improving self-worth and spirituality while decreasing self-centeredness. For example, the Total Life Recovery program may be better equipped to target the matters of the heart and mind (soul) where individuals get in touch with their moral conscious, gain self-respect, and respect for others. Equipping TLR with a larger program could mean assistance for more inmates. When other components are integrated (i.e., transitional case management and licensed practitioners), its added benefits may be available for the transition of inmates back to the community while reducing the rates of recidivism.

Incarcerated women leaving an in-prison faith-based program need help with transitional case management services. Such case management service would connect the inmates with the community, faith-based residential programs or organizations with continued case management services. Such programs would also provide a safe environment for women while being fully re-integrated with resolving health, educational, and employment issues. As well as possibly helping women to build healthy relationships and unification with family. Improving the overall effectiveness of this faith-based program may change the outcomes to align with the paroling authority and the criminal justice system issues.

Recommendations for Future Discussions

Recommendations for future study are naturally linked to the limitation of the information provided in this book. Given the challenges faced in collecting material for this book, the future debates must address some concerns and add to the body of knowledge on faith-based spirituality contribution to the rehabilitation of incarcerated women. Funding is critical for conducting future deliberations on the restoration, rehabilitation, and recidivism rates among incarcerated women. Future discussions must explore evidence-based faith-based programs that employ components such as professional social services, case management, licensed counselors, health, employment, and housings holistically. It may also be valuable to conduct this same style of investigation with a larger sample of women inmates or in other states and among women in the general prison population of the prisons.

In conducting future phenomenological discussion and or research needs to be able to control for external environmental variables. For example, the investigator should ensure that a private area is available for conducting interviews and focus groups. Future discussion related to the issues cited in this book will benefit greatly by using a team approach. With the addition of multiple investigators will address any concerns that may arise with coding and transcribing of the information. The overall value of the information will increase the generalizability of the information in this book.

Future discussion should direct attention to consider measuring the levels of effectiveness that spirituality has on self-esteem, confidence, dreams, goals, self-efficacy, and the ability to build moral and Godly relationships with the offender, God, and others. Another recommendation for future discussion would be to conduct studies on recidivism among incarcerated women in faith-based programs about incarcerated women not participating in faith-based programs.

Furthermore, it is recommended to build on this book by conducting future discussion studies using the identified variables found among the emerged common themes such as relationship, attitude, behavior, and transformation. These variables might be explored further by asking, do these variables have any predictive powers that could aid in understanding the psyche of individuals who are at risk for criminal behavior? For example, how does the inability to form healthy or intimacy in relationships affect the attitude and behavior of criminals? An answer to these question may be an excellent starting point for advancing qualitative research in discovering spiritual variables that may enhance the ability to establish measurements for determining effective outcomes in faith-based programs and organizations. There is still a detectable gap in qualitative research on faith-based spirituality and the impact of spirituality on both rehabilitation and recidivism amongst women offenders.

Conclusion

Researchers today often look into factors associated with individuals who are in the criminal justice system. However, relatively limited inquiries look to factors associated with criminals distancing from a criminal lifestyle. My investigation provides a small, but impressive contribution to the body of existing information on rehabilitating women offenders and reducing recidivism amongst incarcerated women in Hawai`i.

This opportunity truly was a phenomenon to explore the lived experiences, opinions, and worldviews of incarcerated women in Hawai`i. A deeper understanding of the phenomenon of spirituality and the role of spirituality in the rehabilitation of these female inmates in Hawai`i are adequate representation. The information analysis yielded four common themes that went to the heart of this undertaking. The textual descriptions given by the women addressed an unusual phenomenon lead question: *What are the lived experiences of incarcerated women in Hawai`i regarding spirituality?*

The textual descriptions provide insight to the above question of spirituality in the building of a relationship with God, supernatural, or mystical divine being. The impact of spirituality among these participants is clearly the lack of a relationship with God or a mystical divine force. Reportedly, Spirituality among the women attending TLR is the condition of the soul having hope or not having hope. Spirituality amongst the inmates provided the change hook to hope for a future life different from the lives they were living. Therefore, My inquiring mind leads to the following question: *What are the lived experiences of incarcerated women in Hawai`i regarding the role of spirituality in their rehabilitation?*

The responses from the women inmates indicated that the role of spirituality had a profound impact in changing their attitudes and behaviors. The role of spirituality addressed the matter or the heart in changing lives and the goal of keeping them out of prison. The inmates' responses strongly suggest their belief of acquiring a relationship with the God gives them the spirit of hope, love, and forgivingness. Then, they can be in right relationship with God, others, and the society. Because of the Word of God, the inmates' embrace hopes as a positive influence in their desires to change, to seek meaning and purpose in their lives. The women believe spirituality and the role of spirituality not only have changed their behaviors but also been instrumental in changing their desires for the way they want to live outside of prison.

This book of information has contributed to the body of literature and to those who will read it. Being incarcerated may be a painful experience. However, it provides the opportunity for divine interventions. Incarceration allows time, stillness, and opportunity for inmates to learn and reconnect spiritually with their soul. The faith-based, in-prison program has brought about the distinctive heart connection psychological change. Furthermore, directing lifestyle changes, sociability, and life meaning for those inmates who participate in the Total Life Recovery.

I must impress upon the criminal justice correctional facilities the responsibility of not only capturing and housing a body of an inmate, but also the mind and soul of those incarcerated in their custody. So, not all prisoners will be receptive to such intervention. However, the substantial evidence indicates female offenders who are non-threatening have shown positive changes in their attitudes and behaviors.

The establishment of larger in-prison faith-based program is evident to assist a bigger population of women offenders. When measured against the number of incarcerated women a program designed for 20 inmates is much too small. Larger programs are needed to make a huge impact in numbers of prisoners who get rehabilitation services.

This project provided information on spirituality, risk factors, and socio-cultural factors of incarcerated women in Hawai`i. Information on this subject appears to be non-existing in the body of knowledge. Consideration should look at addressing these three factors as targets in reforming services and programs that rehabilitate and reduce recidivism. Per the information presented here spirituality and the role of spirituality have a significantly positive effect in the changing the life and circumstance in the lives of the incarcerated women in Hawai`i.

This research project provided information on spirituality, risk factors, and socio-cultural factors of incarcerated women in Hawai`i which appeared to be non-existing in the body of knowledge. These three areas may be addressed as targets in forming relationships that rehabilitate and reduce recidivism. According to the results of this book spirituality and the role of spirituality have a significantly positive effect in the rehabilitation and the lives of the incarcerated women in Hawai`i.

FINAL THOUGHTS

The information you have just read is not suggesting that Spirituality is the cure-all. Spirituality will not make anything happen without cooperating with God and by being honest; having an open mind, and willingness to change one's psyche and heart. My relationship with God has strengthened. The sores and scars of the soul have lessened. As I connected with a local church, I became more and more intimate in my relationship with God. God has given and showed me my purpose in life.

The God of this universe has equipped me to provide physical, emotional, and spiritual assistance to homeless, parolees, and low-income people. It is so satisfying to work as my Lord has with the disadvantaged, addicts, juveniles, criminals and those who are currently living in incarceration. As well as, others who somehow slip through the cracks in our overburdened society justice and social services system.

I have had an expanded arena with unique opportunities to help a diverse group of individuals and families. It is important, as we use a holistic community and service delivery approach; that we work through faith and with faith-based organizations. One cannot only dream of the implementation of innovative methods for "building one life one family at a time, but it also must be accomplished. There surely can't be any harm in equipping and encouraging hurt disadvantaged populations to pursuit restoration, rehabilitation, and transformation to become productive members of society.

It takes compassion (to be a servant) to work with people who wants to change their lives. Yes, programs, curriculums, and funds are a need for this undertaking. I have been blessed with the passion and equipped to work with people who want to change their lives. My desire is to see homes based in faith that practice and teach spirituality to at-risk juvenile boys and girls. I stand faithfully on my faith in God that this will be created and implemented along with the curriculum and securing of funding.

DEFINITION OF TERMS

Below are the operational definitions of terms relevant to the theoretical concepts of this book.

Co-occurring disorders: Co-occurring disorders occur when patients' presentation meet diagnostic criteria for two or more medical, psychological disorders of the Diagnostic Statistical Manual IV-TR (DSM-IV-TR).

Criminals: Criminals are persons committing a crime punishable by imprisonment greater than one year up to the death penalty. Offenses range from the least nonviolent crimes such as tax evasion to the most violent crime such as murder. The severity of the crime determines the length of the sentence (O'Connor, 2001).

Gender-responsive: Refers to the program, practice, or policy that is designed to address specific needs in the lives of women. Research on women guides Gender-responsive literature. Programs focus on pathways which lead women to commit crimes. Programs are trauma-informed, strengths-based, and culturally sensitive (Bloom, Owen, & Covington, 2004). The essence of the term is its importance of recognizing there are gender differences between men and women. These aspects include every aspect of development: psychologically, socially, and those resulting from trauma, culture, and lived experiences (National Resource Center on Justice-involved Women, 2011).

Inmates: Persons incarcerated in a local jail, state or federal prison, or private facility under contract to federal, state or local authorities (BJS. 2010).

Offender: One who offends, especially, one who breaks a public law (AHCD, 1997).

Recidivism: When an individual is arrested following release from prison and is sentenced for a new crime, it is referred to as recidivism. Recidivism is the measure used by most states to gauge the effectiveness of correctional/criminal justice programs. The goal is to reduce future criminal behavior (BJS. 2010).

Religion: Religion connotes a standard belief ritual system. Religion is concerned with sociable and traditional shared sets of principles and practices, a code of conduct, and doctrine. A belief which includes belief in a God as well as rituals and practices designed to support the values and beliefs of the group (Nichols & Hunt, 2011).

Spirituality: Spirituality is concerned with the meaning and purpose of life and with truth and values (Sims & Cook, 2009). Spirituality is essential, potentially creative, and a universal dimension of human experience within the inner awareness of an individual, communities, social groups, and traditions (Sims & Cook, 2009). "It may be experienced, as the relationship with that which is intimately "inner" immanent and personal, within the self and others, or as the relationship with that which is wholly "other" transcendent and beyond the self" (Sims & Cook, 2009, p. 4).

Spiritual maturity: Those who are not novices or who have much experience in spiritual matters are considered "mature." "Solid food is for the mature and by their constant use has trained themselves to distinguish good from evil." (Hebrews 5:13-14, NIV)

Wahines: Translation for a woman, plural women in Hawaiian.

References

Altman, I. &, Taylor, D. A. (1973). Social penetration: The development of interpersonal relationships. New York: Holt, Rinehart & Winston.

Alexis, E. L. C. (2012). More God, less crime: Why faith matters and how it could matter more. Corrections Today, 73(6), 73-73.

Anumba, N., Dematteo, D., & Heilbrun, K. (2012). Social functioning, victimization, and mental health among female offenders. Criminal Justice and Behavior, 39(9), 1204-1218.

Baack, C., Fogliasso, C., & Harris, J. (2000). The personal impact of ethical decisions: A social penetration theory. Journal of Business Ethics 24, 39–49.

Belknap, J. (2010). Offending women: A double entendre. Journal of Criminal Law & Criminology, 100(3), 1061-1097.

Black, D. W., Gunter, T., Allen, J., Blum, N., Arndt, S., Wenman, G., & Sieleni, B. (2007).
Borderline personality disorder in male and female offenders newly committed to prison. Comprehensive Psychiatry, 48(5), 400-405.

Blanchette, K., & Brown, S. L. (2006). The assessment and treatment of women offenders: An integrative perspective. Chichester West Sussex UK: Wiley.

Blanchette, K., & Motiuk, L. L. (1995). Female offender risk assessment: The case management strategies approach. Poster session presented at the Annual Convention of the Canadian Psychological Association, Charlottetown, Prince Edward Island.

Bloom, B., Owen, B., & Covington, S. (2006). Gender-responsive strategies: Research, practice, and guiding principles for women offenders. Washington, D.C.: National Institute of Corrections.

Bloom, B., Owen, B., & Covington, S. (2004). Women offenders and the gendered effects of public policy. Review of Policy Research, 21(1), 31-48.

Brennan, T., Breitenbach, M., Salisbury, E. J., & van Voorhis, P. (2012). Women's pathways to serious and habitual crime a person-centered analysis incorporating gender responsive factors. Criminal Justice and Behavior, (39)11, 1481-1508.

Buell, M., Modley, P., & Van Voorhis, P. (2011). Policy developments in the USA. In R. Sheehan, G. McIvor, & C. Trotter (Eds.), Working with women offenders in the community (pp. 45-71). Plymouth, UK: Willan.

Bureau of Prisons. (2011). Annual determination of average cost of incarceration. (FR Docket No. 2011-2363). Washington DC: Federal Register.

Bustamante, R. M., Nelson, J. A., Henriksen, Jr, R. C. & Monakes, S. (2011). Intercultural couples: Coping with culture-related stressors. The Family Journal, 19(2), 154-164.

Carpenter M. (2009). The capabilities approach and critical social policy: Lessons from the majority world? Critical Social Policy, 29(3), 351-373.

Carson, E. A., & Golinelli, D. (2013). Prisoners in 2012- advance count: Bureau of Justice Statistics. U. S. Department of Justice, Office of Justice Programs, July 2013, NCJ 242467.

Chambers, J. C., Ward, T., Eccleston, L., & Brown, M. (2011).

Representation of female offender types within the pathways model of assault. International Journal of Offender Therapy and Comparative Criminology, 55(6), 925-948.

Chase, A. E. L. (2012). More God, less crime: Why faith matters and how it could matter more. Corrections Today, 73(6), 73.

Combs, T. (2010). Gender-specific programs help women "break the cycle." Corrections Today, 72(6), 30-33.

Conklin. T. A. (2012). Work worth doing: A phenomenological book of the experience of discovering and following one's calling. Journal of Management Inquiry 21(3) 298–317.

Covington, S. (2007). Women and the Criminal Justice System. Women's Health, 17(4). Washington, DC: Jacobs Institute of Women's Health.

Creswell, J. W. (2008). Educational research: Planning, conducting, and evaluating quantitative and qualitative research. Upper Saddle River, NJ: Pearson.

Culliford, L. (2002). Spiritual care and psychiatric treatment: An introduction. Advances in Psychiatric Treatment, 8, 240-261.

Davis, K. B. (1913). A plan of rational treatment for women offenders. Journal of the American Institute of Criminal Law and Criminology, 4(3), 402-408.

Department of Justice (2006). Bureau of Justice Statistics special report: Mental health problems of prison and jail inmates. (NCJ 213600). Washington DC.

Dik, B. J., & Duffy, R. D. (2009). Calling and vocation at work: Definitions and prospects for research and practice. The

Counseling Psychologist, 37, 424-450.

Duvall, J. L., Staton-Tindall, M., Oser, C., & Leukefeld, C. (2008). Persistence in turning to faith as a predictor of drug use and criminality among drug courts clients. Journal of Drug Issues 38(4), 1207-1224.

Elkins, D. N. (2005). A humanist approach to spiritually oriented psychotherapy. In L. Sperry, & E. P. Shafranske, (Eds.), Spiritually oriented psychotherapy (pp. 131-151). Retrieved from EBSCOhost PsycINFO.

Evans, D., & Adams, M. (2003). Salvation or damnation: Religion and correctional ideology. American Journal of Criminal Justice, 28(1), 15-35.

Faust, E., & Magaletta, P. R. (2010). Factors predicting levels of female inmates' use of psychological services. Psychological Services in the Public Domain, 7(1), 1–10.

Ferrell, O. C., & Fraedrich, J. (1994). Business Ethics: Ethical decision making and cases, (2nd ed.). Boston, MA: Houghton Mifflin.

Ferszt, G. G., Salgado, F., DeFedele, S., & Leveillee, M. (2009). Houses of Healing: A group intervention for grieving women in prison. The Prison Journal 89(46). DOI: 10.1177/0032885508325394.

Finlay, L. (2012). Unfolding the phenomenological research process: Iterative stages of "Seeing Afresh." Journal of Humanistic Psychology XX(X), 1-30.

First, M. B. (2005). Mutually exclusive versus co-occurring diagnostic categories: The challenge of diagnostic comorbidity.

Psychopathology, 38(4), 206-210.

Florida Department of Corrections (FDOC) (2007). "Faith- and Character-Based Institutions (FCBIs)." Retrieved on June 30, 2013, from http://www.dc.state.fl.us/oth/faith/ci.html

Fower, D. N., Faulkner, M., Learman, J., & Runnels, R. (2011). The influence of spirituality on service utilization and satisfaction for women residing in a domestic violence shelter. Violence Against Women, 17(10), 1244-1259.

Given, L. M. (2008). Confirmability, In Sage Encyclopedia of Qualitative Research, (p. 13). DOI: 10.4135/9781412963909. Retrieved June 29, 2013, from Sage Research Methods.

Given, L. M. (2008). Credibility, In Sage Encyclopedia of Qualitative Research, (pp. 139-140). DOI: 10.4135/9781412963909. Retrieved June 29, 2013, from Sage Research Methods.

Given, L. M. (2008). Dependability, In Sage Encyclopedia of Qualitative Research, (pp. 209-210). DOI: 10.4135/9781412963909. Retrieved June 29, 2013, from Sage Research Methods.

Given, L. M. (2008). Transferability, In Sage Encyclopedia of Qualitative Research, (p. 887). DOI: 10.4135/9781412963909. Retrieved June 29, 2013, from Sage Research Methods.

Given, L. M. (2008). Trustworthiness, In Sage Encyclopedia of Qualitative Research, (pp. 896-897). DOI: 10.4135/9781412963909. Retrieved June 29, 2013, from Sage Research Methods.

Greenfield, B. H., & Jensen, G. M. (2010). Understanding the lived experiences of patients: Application of a phenomenological approach to ethics, Physical Therapy, 90(8), 1185-1197.

Guerion, P., Harrison, P. M., & Sabol, W. J. (2011). Prisoners in 2010: Bureau of Justice Statistics. U. S. Department of Justice, Office of Justice Programs [revised 02/09/2012].

Hardyman, P. L., & Van Voorhis, P. (2004). Developing gender-specific classification systems for women offenders. Washington, DC: USDOJ, National Institute of Corrections.

Hatton, D. C., & Fisher, A. A. (2008). Incarceration and the new asylums: Consequences for the mental health of women prisoners. Issues in Mental Health Nursing, 29(12), 1304-1307.

Heilbrun, K., Dematteo, D., Fretz, R., Erickson, J., Yasuhara, K., & Anumba, N. (2008). How "specific" are gender-specific rehabilitation needs? An empirical analysis. Criminal Justice and Behavior, 35(11), 1382-1397.

Hernandez, E. F., Foley, P. F., & Beitin, B. K. (2011). Hearing the call: A phenomenological book of religion in career choice. Journal of Career Development, 38(1), 62-88.

Ho, D. Y. F., & Ho, R. T. H. (2007). Measuring spirituality and spiritual emptiness: Toward ecumenicity and transcultural applicability. Review of General Psychology, 11(1), 62-74 The American Psychological Association.

Juhnke, G. A., Watts, R. E., Guerra, N. S., & Hsieh, P. (2009). Using prayer as an intervention with clients who are substance abusing and addicted and who self-identify personal faith in God and prayer as recovery resources. Journal of Addictions & Offender Counseling, 30(1), 16-23.

Kellett, N. C., & Willging, C. E. (2011). Pedagogy of individual choice and female inmate reentry in the U.S. Southwest. International Journal of Law Psychiatry, 34(4), 256-263.

LA Vigne, N. G., Brazzell, D., & Small, K. M. (2007). Evaluation of Floria's faith and character-based institutions. Washington, DC: The Urban Institute.

Leedy, P., & Ormrod, J. (2010). Practical research: Planning and design (9th ed.), Upper Saddle River, NJ: Pearson Education, Inc.

Matheson, F. I. (2012). Implications of trauma among male and female offenders [Editorial]. International Journal of Environmental Research and Public Health, 9, 97-99.

Mayhew, M. J. (2004). Exploring the essence of spirituality: A phenomenological book of eight students with eight different worldviews. NASPA Journal 41(3), 647-674.

McCullough, M. E., & Willoughby, B. L. B. (2009). Religion, self-regulation, and self-control: Associations, explanations, and implications. Psychological Bulletin, 135(1), 69-93.

McDaniels-Wilson, C., & Judson, L. J. (2011). Women behind bars: An illuminating portrait. Journal of the Institute of Justice and International Studies, 11, 129-XI. Retrieved from http://seach. proquest.com/docview/903538420?acoountid+=39364

McPhail, M. E., Falvo, D. R., & Burker, E. J. (2012). Psychiatric disorders in incarcerated women: Treatment and rehabilitation needs for successful community reentry. Journal of Applied Rehabilitation Counseling, 43(1), 19-26.

Moerer-Urdahl, T., & Creswell, J. (2004). Using transcendental phenomenology to explore the "ripple effect" in a leadership mentoring program. International Journal of Qualitative Methods, 3 (2). Article 2. Retrieved June 30, 2013, from http://www.ualberta. ca/~iiqm/backissues/3_2/pdf/moerercreswell.pdf

Moffitt, T. E. (1993). Adolescence-limited and life-course-persistent antisocial behavior: A developmental taxonomy. Psychological Review, 100, 674-701.

Morgan, R. D., Kroner, D. G., Varghese, F., Flora, D. B., Mills, J. F., & Steffan, J. S. (2011). Treating offenders with mental illness: A research synthesis. Law and Human Behavior, 36(1), 37-50.

Moustakas, C. (1994). Phenomenological research methods. Thousand Oaks, CA: Sage Publications.

National Resource Center on Justice-involved Women. (2011). Resource Brief: Achieving successful outcomes with justice-involved women. Washington DC.

Nedderman, A. B. (2008). A Christian spiritual group with female offenders: Impacting hope. ProQuest Dissertation and Theses, 1-424. UMI Number: 3322810.

Nedderman, A. B., Underwood, L. A., & Hardy, V. L. (2010). Spirituality group with female prisoners: Impacting hope. Journal of Correctional Health Care, 16(2), 117-132.

Nichols, L. M., & Hunt, B. (2011). The significance of spirituality for individuals with chronic illness: Implications for mental health counseling. Journal of Mental Health Counseling, 33(1), 51-66.

O'Connor, P. L. (2001). From arrest to trial: The experience of being a family member of an accused felony offender. ProQuest Dissertations and Theses, 1-276. ProQuest Criminal Justice. Pasko, L., & Chesney-Lind, M. (2007). Honolulu's girl's court:

Lessons learned from a process evaluation. Women, Girls & Criminal Justice 8(6), 81 – 96.

Paul, G. (1992). Women's spirituality in prison. Federal Prisons Journal, 3(1), 41-43, 48. Washington, DC: US Department of Justice, Federal Bureau of Prisons.

Proctor, J. (2009). The imprisonment insights of female inmates: Identity & cognitive shifts for exiting a criminal lifestyle. Justice Policy Journal 6(1), 1-32.

Reynold, M. (2008). The war on drugs, prison building, and globalization: Catalysis for the global incarceration of women. NASW Journal 29(2), 72-95.

Roth, L. H. (1986). Correctional psychiatry. In W. J. Curran, A. L., McGary, & S. A. Shah (Eds.), Forensic psychiatry and psychology (pp. 429-468). Philadelphia, PA: Davis.

Salisbury, E. J., & Van Voorhis, P. (2009). Gendered pathways: A quantitative investigation of women probationers' paths to incarceration. Criminal Justice and Behavior, 36, 541-566.

Schmitt, J., Warner, K., & Gupta, S. (2010). The high budgetary cost of incarceration. Center For Economic and Policy Research. Washington, DC, USA. Retrieved on December 22, 2012, From http://www.cepr.net/

Scioli, A., Ricci, M., Nyugen, T., & Scioli, E. R. (2011). Hope: It's nature and measurement. Psychology of Religion and Spirituality, 3(2), 78-97.

Sharma P., Charak, R., & Sharma, V. (2009). Contemporary perspectives on spirituality and mental health. Indian Journal of Psychological Medicine, 31(1), 16-23.

Shaw, M. E., & Hector, M. A. (2010). Listening to military members returning from Iraq and Afghanistan: A phenomenological investigation. Professional Psychology Research and Practice 41(2), 128-134.

Sims, A., & Cook, C. H. (2009). Spirituality in psychiatry. Glasgow, UK: RCPsych Publications.

Slattery, J. M., & Park, C. L. (2011). Meaning making and spiritually oriented interventions. In Spiritually oriented interventions for counseling and psychotherapy (pp. 15-40). American Psychological Association.

Sumier, M. (2006). Faith-based prison programs. [Editorial]. Criminology & Public Policy, 5(3). Retrieved on January 15, 2013, from ProQuest Central.

Swanson, K. (2009). Faith and moral development: A Casebook of a jail faith-based correctional educational program. Journal of Correctional Education, 60(4), 343-358.

Taylor, D. (1968). The development of interpersonal relationships: Social penetration processes, Journal of Social Psychology 75(1), 79–90.

Taylor, D. &, Altman, I. (1975). Self-disclosure as a function of reward cost outcomes. Sociometry 38(1), 18–31.

The American Heritage College Dictionary, (1997), (3rd Ed.). Boston, MA: Houghton Mifflin Company.

Travin, S. (1989). A national perspective on mental health services to corrections. In R. Rosner & R. B. Harmon (Eds.), Correctional Psychiatry (pp. 17-37). New York, NY: Plenum Press.

Van Manen, M. (2004). Lived experience. In M. S. Lewis-Beck, A. Bryman, and T. F. Liao (Eds.), The SAGE encyclopedia of social science research methods, pp. 580-851. Sage Publication, Inc.

Vandenberghe, L., Prado, F., & de Camargo, E. (2012). Spirituality and religion in psychotherapy: Views of Brazilian psychotherapists. International Perspectives in Psychology: Research, Practice, Consultation, 1(2), 79-93.

Van Voorhis, P., Wright, E. M., Salisbury, E., & Bauman, A. (2010). Women's risk factors and their contributions to existing risk/needs assessment: The current status of a gender-responsive supplement. Criminal Justice and Behavior, 37(3), 261-288.

Volokh, A. (2011). Do faith-based prisons work? Alabama Law Review 63(1), 43-95. Retrieved on April 2, 2013, from www.law.ua.edu/pubs/lrarticles/volume

Walton, E. (2007). Evaluating faith-based programs: An introduction from the guest editor. Research on Social Work Practice, 17(2), 171-173.

Ware, N. C., Hopper, K., Tugenberg, T., Dickey, B., & Fisher, D. (2008). A theory of social integration as a quality of life. Psychiatric Services. 59(1), 27-33.

Weinberger L. E., & Sreenivasan, S. (1994). Ethical and professional conflicts in correctional psychology. Professional Psychology: Research and Practice, 22(2), 161-167.

Whitehead, P. (2011). Faith moves mountains and sometimes reduces recidivism: Community Chaplaincy and criminal justice reformation in England and Wales. British Journal of Community Justices, 9(3), 27-40. Sheffield UK: Sheffield Hallam University.

Willison, J. B., Brazzell, D., & Kim, K. (2011). Faith-based corrections and reentry programs: Advancing a conceptual framework for research and evaluation (Report No. 234058). Retrieved from National Criminal Justice Resource Center website: http://www.ncjrs.gov/

Wolff, N., Frueh, B. C., Shi, J., Gerardi, D., Fabrikant, N., Schumann, B. E., & Phil, M. (2011). Trauma exposure and mental health characteristics of incarcerated females self-referred to specialty PTSD treatment. Psychiatric Services, 68(8), 954-958.

Yamane, J. K. (2011). Management audit of the department of public safety's contracting for prison beds and services (Report No. 10-10). Honolulu, HI: Office of the Auditor. Retrieved from www.ncsl.org/Portals/1/documents/nlpes/pds2011session12yamane.pdf

About the Author

Shirley J. Davenport, Psy. D. was born in Greenville North Carolina. Shirley Davenport earned a B.A. in Psychology, an MSW. in SocialWork from the University of Hawaii at Manoa, and a Psy. D. inPsychology from the University of the Rockies School of Organizational Leadership.

Shirley Davenport is the founder, President, and Psychologist of FOR LIVING HOPE DAVENPORT, LLC. FOR LIVING HOPE offers individuals personal growth, coaching, and counseling recovery services. FOR LIVING HOPE, offers an in innovative prison curriculum over 40 hours of cognitive behavior, rational, emotional, and spiritual development therapy in group instruction and group process for incarcerated men and women in the local, federal, and state correctional faculties.

Having immersed herself in Hawaiian culture, Shirley Davenport received a scholarship to study hula under Kumu Hula Halau: Olana A`i of Palisade. Currently employed as a professor of Developmental Psychology at the University of Hawaii West O`ahu campus and Social Worker at the River of Life Mission, Dr. Shirley Davenport helps provide physical, emotional, and spiritual assistance to the homeless and low-income individuals and families. Dr. Shirley Davenport is

a veteran of the United States Navy and has worked with recovering alcoholics and drug addicts for more than 30 years. She is also a certified substance abuse counselor. With more than 35 years as a resident of Hawaii, Dr. Shirley Davenport makes her home on the island of O'ahu with her husband, retired Navy veteran Calvin Davenport and their dog Piniki. Inside Hawai`i Prison Walls is her second book. You may visit her on the web at www.forlivinghope.com.